Crossing Over

Facing the Challenge to Cross Over into Your Promised Land

Paul Scanlon

Sovereign World

Sovereign World Ltd
PO Box 777
Tonbridge
Kent TN11 0ZS
England

All Scripture quotations are taken from the New International
Version unless otherwise stated. Copyright © 1973, 1978
International Bible Society. Published by Hodder & Stoughton

Quotations marked NKJV are taken from the New King James Bible
© Thomas Nelson Publishers Inc. Nashville, USA

AV – Authorised Version, crown copyright.

ISBN 1 85240 325 X

The publishers aim to produce books which will help to extend and
build up the Kingdom of God. We do not necessarily agree with
every view expressed by the author, or with every interpretation of
Scripture expressed. We expect each reader to make his/her
judgement in the light of their own understanding of God's Word
and in an attitude of Christian love and fellowship.

Typeset by CRB Associates, Reepham, Norfolk
Cover design by CCD, www.ccdgroup.co.uk
Printed in England by Clays Ltd, St Ives plc.

Contents

PART 1

Crossing Over – What Is It and How Do You Do It?

Introduction

This book is the product of a journey. A journey we traveled together as a leadership team and church family. A journey that was expensive. It cost us friends, we were frequently misunderstood and told we would never make it. It was a journey from being one thing to becoming quite another! But it is a journey we successfully made and now continue to travel as we press on towards the goal of fulfilling God's purpose for our lives while we have breath to do it.

The journey took me as Senior Pastor, my leadership team and the whole of the Abundant Life Church here in Bradford, from being a comfortable, predominantly middle class, financially secure, 'good' church, to being an outreach center to the local community and a resource center for Christians across the world. Our growth has been incredible, the mix of people in our church today is as diverse as the cosmopolitan city we live in. Our ministries have multiplied and our 'voice' become one that is in growing demand across the world. And it still amazes and humbles me just to write it in this way!

The start of our journey was incredibly significant. So much so, we called it our 'crossing over.' It was like Israel crossing the Jordan into their Promised Land. There was no going back; the decision to move forward was terminal. It separated them from their past, it took courage, conviction and tenacity, but this is what they had been born for! Not to 'cross over' would have violated God's plan for their lives and put His greater purpose on hold for yet another generation. This is exactly how we felt and today we are living in the good of our determination to cross over, guided by God each step of the way.

The lessons we learned en route have helped many and they have become a significant part of our voice today. It seems that in God's providence, our crossing over has found an echo in the lives of individuals, churches and ministries across the world, and many have thanked us for the insight, help and practical tools gained from our journey. It is for this enduring reason that I have committed to print in this book the key principles from the 'crossing over' period of our journey.

This book is deliberately not written as 'our story' but as a book of principles, illustrated as appropriate by examples from our journey. Each reader is on a unique journey but God's principles of operation are timeless, they have universal application to all who are committed pilgrims. My prayer is simply that from our 'crossing over' you will find inspiration, strength and determination to cross your own Jordan, whatever that may be. The full release of your personal potential and God's purpose for your life depend on it!

Read on, enjoy, and I'll see you on the other side!

Paul Scanlon

Chapter 1

Crossing Over – Part 1

Six steps of preparation
Joshua chapter 1

'Crossing over' is a process that every living, growing, healthy ministry or church will go through at some point. It may be crossing over into a new season of experiencing God's presence, or entering a new type of ministry that God has called you to. Such 'crossings' nearly always require major change, which can be unsettling at best, and traumatic – even devastating – at worst. But crossing over cannot be avoided; to try to do so would be to stifle the growth that God has planned for you and to abort His purposes. For that reason, being prepared for the challenge of crossing over is vital. In this chapter, I want to share with you *six steps of preparation for crossing over*, followed by the *six principles of crossing over* drawn from Joshua's experience of crossing over the Jordan (Joshua chapters 1–3).

The *Jordan* represents the barrier that God is calling you to cross over. It represents the transition between where you are now, and where He wants you to be. This might apply to your church or to you personally. It might be crossing over to achieve your God-given dream or destiny; crossing over into a new aspect of your

Christian life – moving into God's *new thing*, where higher levels of effectiveness and productivity are now possible. Crossing over is about transformation. As a church it may mean making radical changes to the life and structure of your church in order to break through to where God is calling you. It could potentially mean great upheaval with some friction. Personally, it nearly always means having a great deal of courage and a firm belief in what God has instructed you to do.

The keys to a successful crossing that I want to share with you have been discovered during our own experiences as a church. A few years ago, God called us to cross over into a completely new dimension of our destiny. I hope the principles we learned on that journey may be helpful to your own. In fact, I must stress the fact that it is *a journey*. There is no way to avoid the challenge and stresses and strains of crossing over. Just focusing on the 'promised land' and preaching sermons about Canaan will not get you there. Singing songs about where you would like to be will not get you there either! At some point the rubber has to hit the road and you must engage with the challenge God has put before you. If you don't you are deceiving yourself and robbing yourself of your destiny in Christ.

Virtual church

Creating warm feelings and a positive frame of mind in people, without challenging them to break out of the ordinary, is a symptom of church in our society. We have created *virtual church*. It's like being in a flight simulator. You get on board, take the controls and fly the plane, but even if you land it perfectly every time, you still haven't actually been anywhere! Churches can create an environment that seems very like the *real thing* by borrowing

stuff 'off the shelf' from other successful ministries who
are already in a place where their church would like to be.
This might include copying a particular style of worship,
or inviting all the 'right' guest speakers from churches
who have already crossed over. The fact is however, you
cannot cross over simply by being around people who
have already crossed over – though this might be an
important part of your own journey and a learning
process. The bottom line is: *you can't cross over on the
cheap.*

A 'crossing over' perspective

As a church, we found out that you can't cross over with
everybody, and in many ways there is never a 'right time'
to cross over. There will be many who just will not
face the challenge and refuse to go on the journey. Few
churches have the courage to cross over, because few
leaders can face the trauma of the change it represents.
Of those who have faced the challenge, few are willing to
talk about it, for fear that they will lose it. For many it
seems that they are touching something so fragile that
they just keep on thanking God that they made it over
the 'Jordan' and they keep praying that for some obscure
reason He doesn't decide to send them back!

This means that, as a leader, many of the people you
are rubbing shoulders with – other leaders – will not be
talking to you from a *crossing over perspective*. It also
means that, as an individual, the majority of your friends
and acquaintances will never have embraced the challenge of change. Most people you meet will not be
speaking from a 'Canaan' perspective, but an 'on the
way to Canaan' perspective, which will be of limited
help to you on your journey. They will not be saying,
'Look! I made it! Let me tell you about the land . . .' More

likely they will be saying, 'I think you should do this . . . you ought to do that . . . you should try going that way . . . If I were you I would do this . . . '

Therefore, it is important that we listen carefully and hear God's voice, to know the direction He is calling us in. God calls us to advance forward to where He is, already waiting for us – just as He spoke to John in the book of Revelation saying, *'Come up here.'* Just like Jesus said to Peter, 'Look, I'm on the water, come and join me', we should also be listening for God's voice beckoning us forward. Never move forward in response to voices in the church, especially those who are pushing and shoving you, just listen for God's call to proceed.

It is not until we come to the point of crossing over that breakthrough comes. Lives change, commitment is tested and you move beyond the point of no return. Some reading this will not be past the point of no return yet. The point of no return is the place where it is harder to go back than it is to finish the journey; when all your options have gone and you've burnt all your bridges; there's no way out and there's no Plan B. Although you may feel trapped and in a corner, this is actually a positive place to be. God has got you where He wants you. Whatever has gone on before no longer matters. You have arrived at the place where you have no choice but to proceed.

Six steps of preparation

During our own journey, God taught us six things which prepared us for crossing over. If you do these six things you will be left with no other option than to cross over, so if you are not prepared to finish the whole journey, stop here! Whatever you do, don't try to complete one or two of the steps and abort the mission, blaming God for your failure. Think through each step carefully and then take them in sequence.

1. Separation – 'Moses is dead!'

Joshua 1:1 tells us of Moses' death. For God's people to complete the next phase of their journey, God deemed it necessary to bring one term of leadership to a close and to initiate a new one. There had to be a 'separation' – a severing of the things of the past, in order to grasp the future. *Separation is the first act of possession.* If you want to receive something then you've got to let go of something first. It is a life-principle. Therefore the first thing you need to do in order to cross over, is to separate yourself from all the 'stuff' that you cannot take forward with you. You can't have Canaan *and* keep Moses. Consider, what are the 'Moses traditions' that belong to your past? What are the things that are part of your history but are irrelevant and should be long dead? Possible targets could be needless bureaucracy, meaningless church programs that haven't worked for a long time, or anything that the church keeps on doing for no real reason.

You've probably already worked out that if you begin to tamper with these things and make radical changes to you church structure, that some people will leave. That's a sad truth, but it is pointless trying to hold on to people who don't want to go on the journey with you. Release them and send them on their way with your blessing. It may also be that God is breaking a spirit of control that abides in so many churches. However good things have been previously – and there will have been many good and positive things – the old regime has had its day. Those things were relevant in their day, but they have long since passed away – it's just that nobody noticed until now.

God said to Joshua, 'The first thing you've got to realize is that you cannot lead these people the way Moses did.' God knew that most of the people had not grasped this fact, but nevertheless they could no longer function under the old regime with its old mindset. God did not want Joshua to live in the shadow of Moses. Moses' death symbolized a separation from the previous way of doing things and all it represented. This is the challenge that faces you too if you are committed to crossing over and possessing all that God has in store for you.

2. Confirmation

The second step of preparation is *confirmation*. After God brought about a *separation* from the old way of doing things through Moses' death, He confirmed Joshua's position as leader. He affirmed, 'You're the man! You are My choice.' In preparation for crossing over, God has already identified those who are able to go forward and provide a lead that others can follow. Somebody will be the leader to help steer the people in the right direction – or it may be a leadership team which can guide them to the promised land. These are the people who can *smell* Canaan already; they can *taste* it now, even *see* it, though they are not there yet.

God said to Joshua 'I will be with you, I will never leave you, I will never forsake you.' With these words God confirmed Joshua's leadership. He gave him the stamp of approval. God made it clear He was *with* Joshua – not less than He was with Moses, not almost as much as He was with Moses, but with Joshua *just like He was with Moses*. You too need to realize that *God is with you*. You need to know the divine *confirmation* of God. When God speaks to you in this way, you know that you have what it takes and you will be prepared to move forward.

3. Courage

The next requirement for making a successful crossing is *courage*. On the journey there will be many difficulties, challenges and pain, and in order to have your break-through and reach your dream you will need much courage. God majored on this topic with Joshua: 'Be strong ... be courageous ... be strong and very courag-eous ... do not be terrified ... do not be discouraged' (Joshua 1:6–9). Why did God need to tell Joshua so many times? Because He knew what an important ingredient courage would be to Joshua's mission – and how destructive *discouragement* can be. If God tells you something over and over again, it must be because it is *very, very important*! You will need a great deal of courage in order to cross over, because it could be terrifying – literally!

There is a kind of terrorism in the Church. People will try to terrorize you with predictions of what will happen if you try to change. They will try to terrorize you with the consequences of saying certain things from the plat-form; they will tell you that people will leave, that there will be no more tithes and offerings and that con-sequently you won't be able to pay the church's bills. In the face of all of this you need courage.

We have discovered great courage as a church through our crossing over journey. We had to have great, great courage. Please realize that courage itself will not save you, but it will get God involved in saving you, because God likes courage. Look at the list of God's heroes in Hebrews 11. It is not a list of great holy people, but of people who had incredible courage. On that list are a number of people that 'holier-than-thou' Christians would not want in their church! One was a prostitute, one was a murderer, a deceiver, a schemer. There are some pretty undesirable characters in there. But fortunately

Hebrews 11 is not meant to illustrate that if you live a perfect life, God will be able to use you. Rather, it tells us that God is looking for those with the courage to follow Him regardless of the consequences – and that sometimes, in spite of your lifestyle, God will still use you if you have faith and courage.

Courage however, seems to be a rare commodity – especially in the European Church – which is why so many churches are going nowhere fast. The average church in the UK has 20–30 people in attendance on a good day, downhill and with a following wind! We need a lot of help and lots of courage. We also need to be more honest about where we are at than ever before. We have been kidding ourselves for too long about the state of our churches. I believe God is helping us to look at ourselves more honestly in these days and is developing new models of church that will be a breath of fresh air to the emerging generation in our nation.

4. Commitment

God chose Joshua as Moses' successor, He affirmed him, and set him apart as the leader who would help the people cross over. Then God said to him, 'Now watch what I will do in the heart's of the people.' Shortly after, the people came to Joshua and said, 'We are with you' (Joshua 1:16). They said that whatever Joshua commanded, they would do; wherever he sent them they would go. God's *affirmation* of Joshua was followed by a *confirmation* in the hearts of the people. The people showed their commitment to Joshua and committed themselves to follow him on the journey.

The same process of commitment is essential to the success of your journey. The people need to trust that you are God's chosen leader who will take them into their new beginning.

5. Secrecy

It may sound surprising at first, but secrecy is an essential step in the crossing over process. When God is calling you forward into something new, it is all too easy to talk about it too soon to the wrong people and create a nightmare situation for yourself. Afterwards you wish you hadn't spoken so soon, or wish you hadn't said so much. Joshua recognized the need for secrecy. He had the benefit of forty years of distilled wisdom, gained during his time in the wilderness. He had been a part of the first spying mission which had ended in failure. He was a key player in that event, so imagine his frustration at having to abort the journey into the promised land because of the unbelief of others. Imagine how he must have said to himself, 'If I get my chance, I will do *that* differently.'

Moses sent his spies out very publicly, but Joshua decided to do it in secret. The whole nation waited with baited breath for Moses' spies to return with their report. Imagine the speculation that must have been going on while the spies were away. In the same way, there will be endless discussion and speculation in the church if your plans to cross over are aired prematurely. Joshua must have said to himself, 'I will never make that mistake. We need to keep it a secret.' And that is what he did when his turn came.

At the beginning of crossing over, more things will get done by secret arrangement than by public announcement. Saying too much too soon will create problems and cause much instability. In fact, sometimes you have got to operate by stealth on your journey. Thundering announcements and prophecies from the church platform will not win the commitment of the people. You have to able to keep a secret and work in anonymity. Choose carefully the people who you share information with. Initially, you must only work with people who *see what you are seeing* – regardless of who they are. Look for allies who have a corresponding heart, begin to speak to them and fellowship with them. Be strengthened by them and a strength to them. If you can do this, then when the time is right to reveal the plans for crossing over, you will already have a strong immunity against the negativity, criticism and unbelief of others.

The bottom line is, guard your heart, be careful who you speak to and what you say. Don't allow yourself to be hijacked by the opinions of others. Secrecy is an important key. We will explore this in more detail in Chapter 4.

6. Favor in the city

To have *favor in the city* – that is, in your own geographical area – it is critical for churches who desire to cross over, because the city is your future church. Imagine this, most of the people who are your 'church' aren't even saved yet! Your church is the thousands of people who don't even know you exist. God gave Joshua a sign, that the people in the city who feared God were in fact willing to risk their lives, more than some of his own people would risk their lives, in order to make the crossing. God raised up unusual allies in the city in order to bring about His purpose. He gave Joshua Rahab the prostitute – not the governor, or the mayor of the town council.

We need to reverse our thinking on how we take a city. Cities are changed from the grass roots up, not from the top down. You need friends in low places to take a city. Every politician understands this. If a politician can get to the grass roots of a country, he will win. You may want favor with the rich and famous, but all they are going to do is finance your campaign. In order to win an election you need to win the votes of the grass roots electorate.

God gave Joshua favor in the city through Rahab. No doubt most people in the city thought of her as the dregs of society, yet this woman must have told the spies things that they could never have known. She told them what the King was thinking; she told them what the government of the city was saying; she told them what the word was on the grapevine. How? Let's face it, she had probably slept with many of them and knew all the stuff that even people in high positions of authority didn't know. Pillow talk is always far more intimate than around-the-table discussions. This woman was in the loop. Because of her lifestyle, she knew things. She told the spies what she knew, and the spies reported back to Joshua. That must have done something very affirming in his heart. He must have thought to himself, 'There is favor in this city; we have allies here who fear God.'

Your favor is out there too. God has already gone before you as He promised He would. You now need to look for the signs of His favor in your city before you can go and take the city itself. What is the 'city' saying in regard to the dreams you are incubating? How will the city respond when you begin to cross over? One of the initiatives we began as a church was a bus ministry. We now send out buses to bring in people from all over our city. But to start with we tested the water and received an overwhelming response from the people; our city wanted this ministry. It has since broken our church out of its confinement. Now it is not so much 'the church in the city', as 'the city in the church'. You can't tell where one stops and the others starts. This is how it's meant to be!

A few years ago I realized that our church was not reaching the lost. It dawned on me when I observed the number of bags, car keys, mobile phones and other belongings that were left unattended during Church each Sunday. When we started busing people in and one or two things went missing, it was remarkable how quickly that changed! I thought, 'Hallelujah!' because our church was being kicked out of its comfort zone. We were all just too comfortable with one another. Next Sunday, take a look at the floor of your church and judge for yourself where you are at! The unsaved will teach you more about yourself than any Christian. They will force you to actually *be* what you are singing about, instead of just paying lip service to it. All of these potential problems are good problems, because we must realize that a lot of stuff in the church needs to change. Our comfort zones need to be disturbed.

So, our sixth step in preparation for crossing over is to gauge the response of the city and look for God's favor in it. Some of you are seeking favor with the local council, governors and business people, but most of these are not going to do anything for you. They may tell you they will, but few have little intention of doing so. Only reaching the grass roots will help you take a city.

Consider these six steps of preparation carefully, thinking and praying about how you can use them to prepare for your own crossing over. You are then ready for the practical challenge, the challenge of actually crossing over into your promised land. So, buckle your seat-belt and let's consider the *six principles of crossing over*.

Chapter 2

Crossing Over – Part 2

Six principles of crossing over
Joshua chapter 3

After the preparation comes the time to step out and begin your journey, a journey that will successfully reach its destination if you will proceed in the light of the following six principles of crossing over.

In my Bible Joshua 3:1 is subtitled *Crossing the Jordan*. Crossing over requires Joshua leadership. The name Joshua means *savior* and I don't think that is without significance when it comes to crossing over. Moses can get you out of Egypt, but you are going to need a Joshua to get you into Canaan.

Through salvation God is not simply saving us *from* something, He is saving us *to* and *for* something. Many Christians – and therefore many churches – have settled for a 'where we have come from' brand of Christianity. They are more in touch with their sin, their forgiveness, and the journey they have been on, than with what God wants for their future. Instead of realizing what they have become in Christ, they are trapped into thinking about how unworthy they are and what rotten sinners they are. People are often living much nearer to the place they began than the place God wants them to get to. But we should not hang around on the borders of Christianity. A border is simply a place that you pass *through* to enter a new land. No-one who travels into a new country hangs around at the border – they go and explore!

The Apostle Paul expands on this idea constantly as he seeks to help believers grasp the reality of their 'new creation in Christ.' The fact that we have been born-again for a purpose runs through all of his teaching. To learn to live in the 'promised land' of your purpose in Christ you will need Joshua leadership, because Joshua leadership is *possessing* leadership; it is a *land-taking* leadership; it is a *saving* leadership.

Study the journey of any church that has broken through to a new level of God's blessing and provision and you will be reading a story similar to our own. It may have its own twists and turns, different dynamics, but the essence of the journey will be the same – they will have put into practice, knowingly or not, the six principles that we will examine now.

1. Recognize that by crossing over you are 'saving' the church

Sometimes a leader will come to the point where he takes difficult decisions in order to 'save' his church. It means doing what God has told you to do despite popular opinion. It means seeing the bigger picture of what God is calling you to. You have to realize that you are carrying things that will ultimately 'save' people's lives. By crossing over you are releasing them from a death sentence – a fruitless existence in a dead-end church. You have got to be at peace with that and live with the consequences, because you can be sure that you will be misunderstood by many. It is an awesome responsibility. Remember too that crossing over must be something done only in response to a command from God – it is not something to engage in lightly. When the bullets start flying you need to know that God has spoken to you. Joshua leadership 'saves' and by leading with clarity and courage, you will help your church to walk into God's purposes.

2. The ark is not as supernatural as the cloud, because it's time to grow up

Before the children of Israel crossed over and entered the borders of Canaan, they had for a long time been guided by supernatural signs provided for them by God – the cloud by day and the pillar of fire by night. Imagine living your life dependent upon those outward manifestations to know which direction God wanted you to go in, and then suddenly they stop. Until then, all they had needed to do was follow. If the cloud went that way – they went that way.

The cloud was made by God and moved by God. The Ark of the Covenant that they carried with them however, was man-made and was moved by man. The ark did not move by itself, it was carried by selected leaders. I believe that God ceased guiding them by the cloud and the pillar because He wanted to teach them that, if they were to enter their future purposes, they could not do it by following signs. They needed to grow up. God had anointed a leader for them and they were to follow that leader. In the same way, I believe many churches will make little progress until they escape 'cloud-dependent' Christianity and learn to follow the leaders that God has raised up and anointed amongst them. We should be encouraging Christians to get out of the 'heavenly cloud' mentality and begin supporting the leaders that God has invested His anointing in 'on earth'. To cross over therefore requires a maturity of faith that allows us to follow leadership that is carrying God's presence, is going in God's direction and has God's commissioning.

What I have just written will present a huge problem for many, especially British people. There is something in British culture that is fundamentally suspicious, mistrusting and nervous about following a man. Americans do it without thinking about it. 'Yes, and see how gullible they are ... ' you might say. 'Look at Jim Bakker and Jimmy Swaggart.' True, there have been many scandals all across America, but do you know what I would rather have? I would rather risk following a leader who might fail, rather than not following a leader for fear I may be exposed to his human weakness and become disillusioned. Of course we must never overemphasize man rather than God – the leader can never take God's place, he is only God's servant – but God has invested His anointing in men.

'We are following God not men,' is the justifying cry of many Christians today. But this is often a cop out, an excuse to opt out of following the leader or leaders God has appointed. If you are going to cross over into your God-given destiny, you need to leave such airy-fairy points of view behind and get real! The truth is that many would just prefer to float around with the clouds than get behind their leader and support him through the tough times until they really possess the promised land together. The trouble is, there are plenty of clouds up in the sky for those who choose to go that way! Which one will you follow!? Some people are constantly looking for a cloud to guide them – a prophecy cloud; a sermon cloud; a conference cloud – take your pick. I believe God is saying it is time to commit to your leadership – the leadership that will help you to cross over into your destiny in Christ.

We need our churches to move away from 'cloud Christianity' and come to a place of trusting the leaders whom God has appointed to carry His presence. Watch the men carrying the ark of God and follow them. If that doesn't happen, then we will not see vibrant, living, growing, moving churches established that will impact our nation and beyond.

3. *You are on your own for the first thousand yards*

God instructed the people of Israel to keep a distance of a thousand yards between them and the Ark of the Covenant when they crossed over the river Jordan (Joshua 3:8). They were not to get too near it. This illustrates something that I call 'The Leadership Gap'. Jesus modeled this aspect of leadership too. Look at Matthew 26:39 where Jesus was praying with His disciples in the garden of Gethsemane. They spent time together and then the text says that Jesus, '... *went a little farther* ...'. Jesus went on ahead to fall on His face and pray. 'Going a little farther' is what leadership is all about. You are on your own for the first thousand yards – in other words, by the time the rest of the people get to where you are, the breakthrough has already happened. The majority of people who are following your leadership will never see what you saw, feel what you felt, struggle with what you struggled with, need the same faith that you needed, or face the agonies or challenges that you faced. As the leader you are like an arrowhead. Everything that comes behind you will never have to penetrate the same level of resistance you did in order to get the breakthrough.

The Leadership Gap paradigm gives us a number of useful insights. In leadership there is always a gap between you and the first person that follows you through. You cannot break through with a crowd; it is not a group booking. Now if you cannot deal with that, then you are not the person who is going to get the job done. There is a loneliness in leadership that is hard to explain. We are not all crying into our tea! But as leaders, even though you have people who are close to you, there is a degree to which you are on your own in seeing what God wants to do, counting the cost personally, and stepping out to begin the work. At first you will be alone, then people will begin to catch up with you. After a while, you will need to hear God again and venture out alone once more. You are always alone for the first thousand yards.

4. Cold feet!

'When you have come to the edge of the water of the Jordan, you shall stand in the Jordan.'
(Joshua 3:8, NKJV)

Speaking through Joshua, God instructed the priests carrying the Ark of the Covenant to enter the Jordan before all the people. They had to go and stand still in the river. In other words, the only people getting cold feet were the leaders! My message to you is: if you are a leader and you've got cold feet about moving forward into the things God has spoken to you about – don't worry about it. It comes with the turf. I had cold feet about embarking on our church's major building project. I had cold feet about having to make major changes amongst our church staff. It meant hiring some people who were behind the vision and firing some people who weren't. That is not easy to do. I've had cold feet about lots of things we've done but still done them.

Feeling hesitant about daunting tasks is perfectly natural and normal. Sometimes you have to overcome intimidation and fear too – fear that asks you, 'What if this doesn't work out?' At times like these leaders have to seek God. Get alone with God and allow Him to fill you with the courage you need to go on. He is able to give you enough courage to overwhelm the fear, and even though you've got cold feet, you will press through to completion.

5. To enter a new flow you must first break the old flow

To enter a new flow you must first break an old or existing flow. In Joshua 3:13 we read,

> *'And it shall come to pass, as soon as the soles of the feet of the priests who bear the ark of the LORD ... shall rest in the waters of the Jordan, that the waters of the Jordan shall be cut off ... and they shall stand as a heap.'*
>
> (NKJV)

God had told the people of Israel that Canaan was a land *flowing* with milk and honey. Between them and that new, flowing land was the *flow* of the river which was in flood at that time.

There is never a 'good' time to cross over. It was as if God had engineered it so that Israel would have to cross over at flood time – so that they would know without a doubt that God was miraculously intervening. Why not cross over in a drought? Because it would not have required much faith on their part to wade through a foot of water. They needed to trust and see God work on their behalf. God is likely to give you confirmation about crossing over only after you have stepped in, which is what happened here. God said to them 'If you are going to get into that land of new flow you are going to have to put your feet into the old flow, and when you put your feet into the old flow, the old flow will be cut off.' All you have to do is wade in, willing to believe that you have heard from God, and He will be there with you immediately, stemming the flow of the river that threatened to sweep you away.

The idea of 'being in the flow' is one that God has spoken to me about often. Every believer needs to learn how to live in the 'flow' of God's will. We have got to get away from the myth that the will of God is a tightrope that we can fall off because of a moment's hesitation or a wrong decision. It is not. God's will for us can often be multiple-choice. Because He has called us His friends, we are often invited to make suggestions – He gives us the option to choose sometimes. Out of a relationship with God like this, our leadership team has made multi-million pound commitments for our church while sitting around eating pizza! We were talking, the TV was on in the corner and and 'boom' we just decided. We didn't have prayer and fasting into the night, or fifteen committee meetings. Why? Because we just knew we were in the flow of God's will. We felt it was right, we were at peace about it. We felt the momentum of God in our hearts. We knew we had done the preparation and that God was giving us a 'green light' of approval to proceed.

6. Leaders must stand firm until everyone has crossed over

Lastly, leaders must keep standing against the old flow until everyone who wants to has crossed over. The leaders are the ones who must hold firm to the vision until everyone is on 'dry ground'.

> '*Then the priests who bore the ark of the covenant of the* LORD *stood firm on dry ground in the midst of the Jordan; and all Israel crossed over on dry ground, until all the people had crossed completely over the Jordan.*'
>
> (Joshua 3:17, NKJV)

Our leadership team had to stand firm for a solid eighteen months, six months of which were pretty hell-ish. We effectively broke a twenty-five year old flow in just two years. To do this you need a lot of commitment, and you must have already decided that you are in for the long haul. To enter into the new thing that God has called you to – that new ministry, new commissioning – then the old flow must be broken. It takes faith and patience.

Remind yourselves of where you have come from

Finally, having embraced the six principles of crossing over, we should take with us a reminder of where we have come from. The Lord commanded Israel to take twelve stones out of the Jordan and set them on the bank as a monument to remind them of their crossing (Joshua 4:8–9). The stones would remind future generations that God was powerful and able to fulfill His promise to take them into the promised land.

Likewise, take some 'stones' with you when you cross over as a reminder of what God has done. What does this mean in reality? Mostly it means talking about the journey you've been on from time to time, reminding the people of God's goodness. This is important for new people who have joined the church more recently. They need to understand the history and what it has cost people to establish the church they are now enjoying.

All the trouble that comes as a result of crossing over is worth it because of what comes next – the promised land. We thank God that we survived our own journey and have since prospered; we lived to stand on the other bank and tell the tale. The old flow has been broken and we shout to everybody on the other bank, 'Come on over, it gets better from now on.'

PART 2

'Crossing Over' Leaders

Chapter 3

People-Possessed

Acts 26

In the following three chapters I want to discuss in more detail some important aspects of the character of the 'crossing over' leader. They are based on lessons that God taught me personally on our journey and these principles didn't come without their pain and challenges. But they are attributes that I believe are critical for leaders who are going to negotiate a successful 'crossing'.

In this chapter I want to examine a particular facet of the Apostle Paul's character – a vital trait of an effective leader. I have studied Paul's life for many years now, and recently as I was reading Acts 26 this particular aspect of his character stood out to me. It may not be immediately obvious from a quick reading of the text, but if we dig a bit deeper we will find one of the keys to the Apostle's incredibly productive life.

Paul left us an incredible legacy. He has made an impact on this world far greater than he could have realized at the time. Though he came to Christ as an adult, he still managed to embark on numerous missionary campaigns, plant a great many churches and write a third of the New Testament before he died. He had a lot of learning to do when He came to Christ and plenty of baggage that he needed releasing from as he describes in Acts 26 – just like most of us.

At the beginning of this chapter, Paul is appearing as a prisoner before King Agrippa who invites him to give account of himself. Paul recalls something of his life and history to the King, and he recounts for the first time what happened on the Damascus road. We read a little of this event earlier on in Acts, but here, years later, Paul tells what happened in greater detail including what the voice said that spoke to him.

> 'Then I asked, "Who are you, Lord?" "I am Jesus, whom you are persecuting," the Lord replied. "Now get up and stand on your feet. I have appeared to you to appoint you as a servant and as a witness of what you have seen of me and what I will show you. **I will rescue you from your own people and from the Gentiles. I am sending you to them** ... "' (Acts 26:15–17)

Verse 17 in the Authorized Version reads, *'I will deliver you from the people unto whom I will send you ...'*

God-centered not people-centered

This is the statement that really stood out to me and highlights a quality Paul had that I believe is so important: *before you can help the people that God sends you to, you first have to be **delivered from people***. God was saying to Paul, 'First I am going to deliver you from people, then I am going to send you to help people.' This is an interesting paradigm.

Most people begin trying to help people before learning to be delivered from people. What do I mean by being delivered 'from people'? It means not being people-driven and people-centered, but God-centered. As a church leader you need to be a person who loves people and who is committed to people. People are your business. But if you allow yourself to be driven by other people then you are in trouble. You will never have a God-centered ministry and you will never make an impact with your life until you have been delivered from the opinions, agendas and expectations of others. For many church leaders today Acts 26:17 reads, 'Having been delivered from God by the people, they went to help the people . . . '

Before you even begin to build a church, establish a ministry, reach a community, or launch an initiative, you need to be focused on God and not the expectations of others. Even if you have a well-established church or ministry it is always a good time to stop and examine where you are at. Over time, even the most God-inspired ministry can subtly shift from being God-centered to people-centered.

Paul writing to the Corinthians said,

> 'Though **I am free and belong to no man**, I make
> myself a slave to everyone, to win as many as possible.'
> (1 Corinthians 9:19)

I believe his statement here is an expression of what God did for him on the Damascus road. 'I belong to no man, but I make myself a slave to as many people as possible.' What you make yourself in order to reach people is one thing, but what people try to force you to be for their own reasons is entirely another. Paul said, 'I am free, no one owns me. Now, because I have my freedom, I can choose – and have chosen – to make myself a slave to others, so that they will be saved and God's purposes will work out in their lives.' In other words it was on Paul's terms; Paul was in control of his ministry under God's headship. People did not control Paul – God did. Sometimes the decisions Paul made and the things he did made him very unpopular with others. He was often severely misunderstood. But this didn't bother Paul, as long as he knew he was in God's will, and he was determined to do whatever God told him to do.

Whether Paul understood what God was doing for him on the Damascus road, I'm not sure. Nevertheless, his lack of concern for the agendas of others and his single-minded pursuit of God's will became the hallmarks of his ministry.

Ask yourself these questions now:

- 'Am I people-possessed or not?'

- 'Have other people caused me to do, or become, something that I wouldn't naturally choose?'

- 'Am I preaching about things in my church that God has not spoken to me about because of people-pressure?'

- 'Have I avoided preaching about something that God has spoken to me about because of people-pressure?'

Empowering others

Is there anyone you know who, when you hear their voice on the phone or bump into them, your heart sinks? Who in your church are you always on the run from? Are there people who make you feel guilty if you don't call them, visit them, or be there for them when they need you?

As members of the Body of Christ we need to love each other and be there for each other. We need to have the freedom to tell other people, 'Hey, I'm really struggling; I need your help ... ' Of course we must do that, but we must not do it in a way that produces guilt in others. Neither is it helpful if we only help others out of a sense of guilt, or out of the fear that they might say something bad about us if we don't.

I say up front to our church that if ever I visit you in hospital, you'd better start choosing the hymns! If you see me walking down the ward, there is something they ain't telling you! I don't do hospital visiting because there are people in the church who are more gifted to do that than I. We have a team who love to do it and it is their forte; they love sitting with people, talking through things and helping them. Most leaders will have done this at some time in their growth and development, but there comes a point when your time is at a premium, when you have to allow others to do the time-consuming things – you can't do it all yourself. As a leader you should be seeking to empower those who have specific gifts to use them where they are needed.

Are you people-possessed?

How many meetings have people got you in that you shouldn't have been in? How many committees do you sit on that God doesn't sit on with you? Do people make you stay in touch all the time so that you feel bad if you haven't been in touch for a while? Are you a leader who keeps your mobile phone on constantly, even when you are meeting with someone else, just in case 'someone' needs you? Do you keep your mobile phone on even when you have gone off to pray and read the Word quietly alone with God? Are you someone who feels that you cannot be 'out of touch,' just in case you are needed for an emergency? Do you subliminally think, 'The moment something happens I just know that I am going to be out of touch and there will be a scandal in the church?' If this is you, then to one degree or another you are people-possessed.

Consider: how many people 'eat dinner' with you each evening? How many people 'go to bed' with you? How many people 'go on vacation' with you? The answer is often you, your spouse, and half the church! Are you afraid to do something that God has told you to do, because if you do it certain people will give you a hard time? How much of your ministry is driven by guilt and duty and how much of it is driven by God and His purposes? Do you drive the kind of car that people make you feel is suitable for a Pastor? Are you wearing clothes that people make you feel you should wear? And what about the way you wear your hair or do your makeup? Is it your choice or to please others? What kind of house do people make you live in? If any of this is ringing bells with you, then you are people-possessed.

These are tricky questions, but they need answering. Where they are not addressed there exists a frustrated, people-possessed leader. It is pastors like this who would not even recommend their own church to someone trying to find a place to attend in their town! Instead they recommend another church where they know the people asking would have less of a hard time! I wonder: to whom in your church would you like to say, 'You are the weakest link. Goodbye!?'

The closing verses of John chapter 2 tell us that,

> *'While he was in Jerusalem at the Passover Feast, many people saw the miraculous signs he was doing and believed in his name. But Jesus would not entrust himself to them, for he knew all men.'*　　(John 2:23–24)

Even Jesus did not entrust Himself to others, because He

knew the hearts of men. He knew that ultimately everyone – even His closest friends – would desert Him.
However, even though Jesus knew that it didn't cripple
Him; it didn't disable Him emotionally; He wasn't filled
with bitterness, knowing that people would come and go
and not be faithful to Him. He knew that even those who
had pledged undying love to Him would turn away from
Him in His hour of greatest need. Jesus knew that, and if
you don't know that then you need to wake up!

Peter had vowed to die alongside Jesus. A few days later
He denied ever having known Him at all. Even so, Jesus
didn't hold any bitterness or grudge towards him. The
Bible says that when Peter denied Jesus, they caught each
other's eyes. I believe that when their eyes met, Jesus
wasn't looking at Peter with a stare of condemnation or
disbelief. Jesus wasn't shocked by this turn of events. His
eyes said, 'It's OK Peter. I am moving on and you will
need to move on too. You are going to have a rough
time, but I am praying for you.' Later we find Peter on
the day of Pentecost standing up and saying to the
crowd, 'You who denied him ...' What a restoration
that enabled Peter to say that! It shows how he had come
through.

Getting free from people-possession

So, how do you get free from people-possession to the
degree that the Apostle Paul was, or as completely liber-
ated as Jesus was? You can start by doing something
small. What I am about to suggest may not immediately
compute for some people, but take some time to reflect
on this: your training as a leader has probably condi-
tioned you to think that leadership is all about giving
100% of yourself to others; denying yourself completely
and being completely available to others. I want to

suggest that there should be a small percentage of 'you' that you never give away to another person, but is only ever shared between you and God. It may be as little as 1% or 2%, but there should be a tiny percentage that is you and God alone, and is not shared with even your wife, husband, or children.

This doesn't make you dysfunctional as a person. It doesn't make you non-trusting or untrustworthy. It simply means that whatever happens in life you have always got something that you have kept that's just between you and God. Hear Paul again when he writes to Timothy saying, 'At my first defense ... everyone deserted me ... but the Lord stood at my side and gave me strength' (2 Timothy 4:16–17). The last part of this statement shows that Paul had something that he never gave to a person.

If you give yourself 100% to people and they walk out on you, they take your 100% with them and leave you bankrupt. Only God is faithful as Jesus knew so well. You need to lead your life in ministry so delivered from people, that whatever they do or say about you doesn't affect you. It does not phase you when they pledge and commit but then don't follow through. Whoever it was and whatever they did doesn't matter and you can still say, 'Well, God stood by me' and move on without bitterness.

A close examination of the Scriptures reveals that even Jesus' family tried to control Him at times, but He refused to be driven by the expectations of others, regardless of their connection to Him. Sometimes it seems that Jesus is being harsh or uncaring towards His family in these instances in Scripture, but He was simply being God-centered and God-focused, intent on doing only what the Father showed Him without worrying about how it might appear to others.

People-possession cost Moses his destiny and it could

cost you yours too. Remember the occasion when God said to Moses that he should go out and speak to the rock, so that water would gush out of it? When Moses went out in front of the people they were so whiney and negative that it wore him down and Moses lost it for a split second. He whacked that rock twice in his anger and then took the credit for it rather than giving it to God (Numbers 20:10–12). God said 'talk to it', not 'whack it.' Now, if God says whack it, you whack it, but if God says talk to it, you talk to it. Sometimes people will get you so frustrated that you just want to pick up the stick when God is saying, 'No you're going to manage this one just by speaking to it in the Spirit.' (Sometimes things just need to be dealt with in prayer without making a big fuss or having a confrontation.) Moses lost it because the people so aggravated him and he belted that rock. God said to him, 'Because you have dishonored me in the way that you handled this, you will not go into the promised land.' What a terrible thing, not least because Moses loved those people to a fault. The sobering lesson is that if you are people-possessed you can love people to such a degree that they get to enter in and God keeps you out! This is shocking, but it's important.

So, you need to begin today to become free of people-possession. You don't have to make an announcement or a scene about it. The uncoupling can take place inside you without anyone visibly noticing at first. Eventually though, people will know that something has changed – there is a difference about you, about your church, your ministry. You will become more productive and fruitful than you have been for years. Ask God to reveal to you where you have allowed people to control you instead of the Holy Spirit. Pray quietly that God will help you to become free. Ask Him to help you progressively get to that place where you will do whatever He asks you to do without worrying about the consequences. Ask God to help you be yourself. I have discovered something in life: there is always somebody that can do what you do better than you can do it. But no one is better at being you than you! You may even need to discover with the Holy Spirit's help who 'yourself' is. But it is conquering the bondage of people-possession that will help you to cross over into the fullness of all that God has for you. Make a start today!

Chapter 4

Secret Keepers, Devil Beaters

Joshua 2:1

I now want to take you back to the early chapters of Joshua which we have been examining in order to help us identify the stages involved in 'crossing over the Jordan' into our God-given destiny. These passages of Scripture helped us greatly on our own journey as a church. As we walked that journey, we had to change our thinking, our agenda, our vision and our values. We had to change our relationships and the way we have done things historically. The challenges that Joshua faced and the crossing of the Jordan by the people of Israel have certainly helped us understand many of our own experiences.

Back in Chapter 1 of this book we identified one particular lesson that Joshua learnt which I believe will be especially useful for all leaders planning the future shape of their church – it was the preparatory step of secrecy.

> *'Then Joshua son of Nun secretly sent two spies from Shittim. "Go, look over the land," he said, "especially Jericho." So they went and entered the house of a prostitute named Rahab and stayed there.'*
>
> (Joshua 2:1)

The wilderness years

These verses represent forty years of distilled wisdom. This was *deja vu* for Joshua. Forty years earlier he had been part of the first, aborted attempt to enter Canaan. He had not just tried to enter as one of the people of Israel, he had also been sent to scout the land as a spy. He knew this game from both sides. Joshua had been there, done it and got the T-shirt! The difference this time was that forty years on, Joshua had had plenty of time to think things over. He had not had a lot to do during that time – wandering around the desert; years of sleepless nights mulling it over; endless conversations with Caleb about how they might have handled things differently. Last time Moses was in charge. Now it was Joshua's turn and he had an opportunity to do things differently.

Joshua 2:1 speaks to me of lost youth. Joshua's lost youth; a nation's lost youth. It must also represent countless graveside good-byes to everyone Joshua ever knew of the previous generation who died in the wilderness – extended family, distant relatives, close personal friends – all of them perished in the wilderness rather than the promised land, and Joshua watched them die. It is estimated that Israel had an average of 90 funerals per day to bury the wilderness generation. Hundreds of thousands perished without realizing their destiny because of one day when the spies returned home and said, 'We cannot possibly take this land.' The forty day trip to Canaan became a forty year death sentence to a generation because of hard-heartedness and unbelief.

God drew my attention to this verse and said to me, 'Stop, look and learn.' I realized that Joshua 2:1 is no incidental statement written simply to get us to the next 'important' part of the story. This short statement shouts out to us of Joshua's deep desire to put right what had previously gone terribly wrong. He was itching for the time when he could correct the wrong of forty years and countless lost lives. The key word in this verse is 'secret'. Hence the title of this chapter, because secret keepers are devil beaters.

There are two fundamental things that Joshua waited all his life to do differently than Moses. He said to himself, 'If only Moses had kept it all a secret, we could have entered the promised land.' Unfortunately, Moses had announced to the whole nation that he was sending spies to scout the land, and had then chosen famous tribal leaders to carry out the mission. They are all named in Scripture. It was all done with great proclamation and publicity. If only it had been done secretly with a couple of specially chosen people that no one knew well, it would have been a different story.

Secrecy and anonymity

So, the second time around Joshua decided that he needed to operate in both *secrecy* and *anonymity*. This time no one knew what was going on – so they couldn't get involved in it – and the spies that were chosen for the mission were just 'men' that the Bible says little about. The wisdom of forty years said, 'If you are going to invade a land the key is to begin in secret, and if you are going to take cities, then it is better done by "faceless" soldiers than "famous" warriors.'

How can we apply this principle to our own experiences of crossing over? The lesson to learn here is, *private arrangement is better than public announcement.* As leaders it is often preferable to 'keep secret' things concerning the future of the church while we incubate ideas and weigh up the possible alternatives. It is nearly always better to speak when you have a well-formulated plan, rather than speaking publicly when plans, thoughts or ideas are in their infancy. From a purely logical point of view this makes sense, but it is important for another reason too. Joshua knew that from the moment he spoke out his plans, everything would be different. The moment you speak out, everything changes and you must be prepared for that.

Everything that God does begins in secret. Every natural birth begins that way, so we should not be surprised that every spiritual 'birth' begins that way too. When you were conceived you were hidden in your mother's womb. For a while, even your mother didn't know you existed. You were God's best kept secret. No one saw your unformed frame except Him. Later when the physical evidence of pregnancy appeared, it became obvious to everyone. Similarly, the spiritual conception begins as a secret shared only with the Lord, and grows inside until eventually the pregnancy becomes apparent and an announcement is then appropriate. I guess that many reading this book will have 'secret pregnancies' – dreams or desires of achieving something for God – things that as yet are a secret between you and God. What is it that you are carrying in your heart that only He knows about? If it is not long since it was conceived, then let it grow and develop within you. We need to realize that existence preceded conception. Pray it through. Allow God to bring it to birth at the right time.

At one of our regular staff social evenings, we once did a little exercise both for fun and to help us get to know each other better. Everyone had to write down on a piece of paper a secret from their past that no one else knew about. All the papers were collected in and one person read out all the secrets. We had to guess which secret belonged to which person. We asked ourselves, 'Who would be capable of doing that?' It was a real shocker! Who would have thought that one of our staff was kicked out of Sunday school when they were young for being naughty – and was so angry about it that they stood outside the door banging and kicking it and swearing! Another, who was a secret Star Trek fan, had skipped meetings to stay at home and watch it! But of course this was all a long time ago!

Keeping a secret with God

God works with people who can keep a secret. The Bible says in Psalm 25:14,

> 'The LORD confides in those who fear him.'

Think of someone who you would never ever dream of telling a secret to. You shouldn't have to think too hard. All of us know people who, if we told them our deepest secret, they would have it spread around the world by sun down! Now think of someone who you wouldn't hesitate to tell a secret to – someone who you know you could confide in and it would go no further. The qualities that the second group of people possess, are the same qualities that God looks for to see who He can confide in. Throughout history God has confided in people who have shown a deep respect and fear of Him. In those 'secret places' of confidence great moves of God have quietly and secretly been incubated into fullness.

When a thing is a secret it belongs exclusively to God and that person. Only God knows about it. God is the only person you can talk to about it, and only God can talk to you about it. There is a divine exchange that is locked up, secret and special, untainted by human touch.

It is apparent in the Bible that from the earliest time God confided in men and it created a special bond between Him and His servants. A secret is an expression of trust that is rare. In these days of openness and communication, everybody tends to know everybody else's business, and the Church is probably the worst company of people in the world for breaking confidences. I doubt that there are many people reading this book who have not at some time been hurt by a betrayal of confidence. People share secrets because they see it as a means of deepening a relationship. It creates a bond of trust and fellowship because you are entrusting something you consider precious to another person. But when that trust is breached, it leaves a wound. Imagine how that can happen to God when He shares precious secrets with us and we carelessly gossip what He has said to all and sundry. If you want to be someone who God confides in, then you have got to learn the discipline of holding on to what is in your heart until it is the right time to tell another person. And when you do, be careful who that person is.

God is drawn to people who can keep a secret. Right now he wants to reveal things to you by His Spirit – things about your destiny, your calling, your dreams and the things you can accomplish for Him. But can you hold them in your heart until the time is right? When Nehemiah went to look at the damage in Jerusalem, the Bible says that the first night he took a donkey on his own and went around the city walls secretly. He told no one what God had put in his heart. Eventually, when the time was right he announced what God had told him (Nehemiah 2:13–16). Do you know that there are secret ways to access your city? There are secret ways for the kingdom of God to infiltrate any city in your country. The key to the city is not what the Lord Mayor hands you, but the key to the city is a strategy, given by God in the Spirit, that will allow His people to break open their town, their city, and even their nation.

I want to make it clear that I am not speaking about keeping secrets that cover up sin, or suggesting that we keep secrets as leaders so that we become elitist. That is bordering on cultist behavior and is where leadership teams begin to go off the rails – where there is no accountability. I am talking about keeping the 'secret of the Lord' which He reveals to those who fear Him. Samson lost his anointing and his life because he couldn't keep a secret from a nagging woman who played a game of emotional blackmail to get him to surrender the secret of his unusual strength. Eventually he gave in, and the moment he told her his secret the anointing came off him (Judges 16:15–20).

Joshua realized that if he was going to conquer Jericho, the last thing he needed was a public fanfare. The last thing we need, if we are seeking to do anything for God in our cities, is big announcements before we even get close to doing something for Him. Let's strategize to take our cities in secret and let's do it through anonymous people. Allow the Lord to share His secrets for the future of your church and hide them in your heart until the right time. Then you will have a powerful foundation from which to see God move in your church.

Secret keepers are devil beaters. What the devil does not know about he cannot contaminate with unbelief, fear and intimidation. The devil cannot read your mind. He does not know what's in your heart. He does not know what you are meditating on until you speak it out. Only then can he listen. So position yourself in the 'secret place' with God so that He can take you to a deeper and more intimate place with Him, and listen as He reveals the secret strategies that will help your church to cross over.

Chapter 5

Tamar Churches and Onan Leaders

Genesis 38:1–30

In the previous chapters I have issued two challenges to leaders who are seeking to take their people over their particular 'Jordan': First, are you people-possessed? And secondly, can you keep a secret? We now move to a third principle which will require you to honestly assess both your leadership and the nature of the church you are trying to 'cross over' at the helm of. I root this in what some may think is an unusual passage of Scripture when speaking about leadership principles. But don't let that put you off because enshrined in this story are some very important principles that will make or break your ability to 'cross over' successfully. The key verse from this passage is Genesis 38:8 which says:

> *'Then Judah said to Onan "Lie with your brother's wife and fulfil your duty to her as a brother-in-law to produce offspring for your brother." But Onan knew that the offspring would not be his; so whenever he lay with his brother's wife, he spilled his semen on the ground to keep from producing offspring for his brother. What he did was wicked in the LORD's sight; so he put him to death.'*

The social custom at that time required that, if you died before you had children with your wife, then the next person in line – your brother – would marry your widow and have children for you. In that way your line could continue. I guess in those days it really mattered what the woman your brother married looked like!

The whole passage from Genesis 38:1–30 is an interesting, shocking, cannot-believe-you-would-find-it-in-the-Bible kind of story. If you are not familiar with it, I suggest you read it now. What a story! Incest, prostitution, deceit, lying, abuse, you name it, it's all there! Yet, Judah, Tamar, and the twins that were born to that incestuous, immoral relationship, were all destined to be part of Jesus' messianic family line. Tamar is one of the three women listed in Christ's genealogy who would not be welcome in most churches today – Rahab the prostitute, Bathsheba the adulteress, and Tamar, guilty of an incestuous relationship. All three are mentioned in Matthew chapter 1. Truly, it is by grace are we saved! Grace is an ocean without a shore.

In this chapter I want to challenge you to think about the concept of *Tamar churches* and *Onan leaders*. What are Tamar churches? They are groups of God's people everywhere, sometimes entire churches, but usually a number of people within a church that are desperate to *conceive* and produce spiritual offspring, but they cannot because they are trapped under Onan leaders.

✤ What are Onan leaders? Onan leaders are those who give plenty of stimulation, but no impartation. Onan leaders are leaders who spill their spiritual seed and don't sow it. It is leadership by containment. It is leadership that is fearful to follow through and to put seed into people and invest in their dreams in case they lose control of the outcome. Instead of seed-sowing they adopt a strategy of seed-spilling. It is obvious from the outcome of this story that God takes the spilling of seed very seriously.

Spiritual hype and virtual reality

What the Church can do without today is any more Onan leaders who stimulate, but do not impart anything. To stimulate means to excite, to arouse, to hype-up or titillate. To impart means to hand something over, to pass something on, to bestow something on another person. Stimulation costs nothing, produces nothing and changes nothing, yet there is a huge demand in the church for stimulation. Spiritual hype is very popular; it is trendy and fashionable. Spiritual hype produces meetings where everyone gets tremendously excited, but ends up going nowhere and achieving nothing. Charismatics in particular are brilliant at this!

But hype creates a virtual reality church. Because we get excited it gives us the feeling that we are making progress. Because we are singing about advancing the kingdom we start to believe it – even if we are not. And if we are not advancing the kingdom then all we have in fact, is a circus. It's just stimulation, entertainment; it serves no other purpose.

Stimulation creates a circus, but impartation will build a house for God. Impartation is building material, it means you *give something* away to people in your worship team, in your youth team, in your pastoral ministry. It means that every time you are ministering, or even just hanging out with people, you are handing something over – giving out of your spiritual experiences in order to build them up. You are not whipping them up by stimulation and making them feel good about themselves, but you are passing something to them that will help build their character. Just as when the woman touched the hem of Jesus' garment and He felt power leave Him, you should also feel that you have emptied yourself and given of yourself to others.

Sadly, the Church has perpetuated 'goose bump'

Christianity – even encouraged it. People will readily travel the world just to get a goose bump on top of their goose bumps. To get another exciting prayer-line moment, to be near the great and famous in the body of Christ; to be in a large crowd, to be where the latest spiritual hotspot is. People will travel the world and spend thousands of pounds to do that when they can't even pay their electricity bill. This is a sad indictment on many parts of the Church today.

Building instead of blessing

Hyped-up meetings, hyped-up preaching, hyped-up appeals and hyped-up prophesying gets everyone excited, but actually nothing has changed. No lost have been reached; no church has been built; nobody is leaving with a changed life. I feel very deeply that to build effective churches we must have a 'build the house' mentality, rather than a 'bless the house' one. Unless I pass something on to you, and you leave my church with something more than you came in with, then we haven't had church. Unless you are seeded, and that seed has within it your destiny, or a call, or a gift, or ideas – then you haven't been to church. I say to our church every Sunday, 'If I can't give you something that you can use before you hit the car park, you should ask for a refund.'

Your ministry should be so relevant that you don't ever need to wonder what it is all about. If you are a leader who only ever stimulates people and never imparts anything to them, then you should apologize to your congregation now and go and get yourself another job. I get weary of shouting, bawling, spitting, perspiring preachers – numbers of whom are on TV – who speak for a long time and still leave you wondering to yourself, 'What in the world have they just said?' The answer: nothing, absolutely nothing. You would think that with all the shouting that something important had been said. But mostly it is an empty message dressed up with drama, perspiration, and volume with a few unendingly repeated Bible verses thrown in. When you hear messages like these, ask yourself, 'What has been passed on to me that will help build my life, shape my character and deepen my roots in Christ? Has this equipped me as a believer?'

People in the Body of Christ need equipping. They have needs. They want to know what will help them to reach higher spiritual ground. They want answers to the problems they face in their marriages, health and finances. But Onan leaders simply stimulate and send them back out into their spheres of life as ill-equipped to live a victorious Christian life as when they came in.

Tamar believers

I have met Tamar Christians all over the world. Let me tell you what Tamar does. She creeps in at the back of a conference or church hoping that no one will recognize her. She is drawn to that place because it has an atmosphere of conception, and she has come with one agenda – she's not leaving until she's pregnant. That's a Tamar, and every church has them. Tamar Christians are so desperate to conceive – to experience the reality of God – that they will go looking for a spiritual 'one night stand' with some stranger in the pulpit. Tamar Christians go to meetings for one reason only: they are waiting for something to be said that will change their lives, so that they can leave the meeting 'pregnant' with destiny.

Tamar Christians are so desperate to conceive that it is nothing short of a tragedy when they are stifled by seed-spilling Onan leadership. Onan 'inherited' Tamar because he was next in line, but because he had no interest in making her pregnant, Tamar took a reckless course of action to achieve her goal. Tamar broke free of the restraints of the custom and tradition she was born into. Custom and tradition often fail to get the job done in our churches too. It's not that they shouldn't be observed or respected, but tradition in and of itself cannot seed a person's life. People today are no longer so loyal to the traditions and heritage of the past. They simply say, 'Give me some seed or I'll die.' And if you're not providing the seed they will go looking for it elsewhere.

What Tamar did to get pregnant was indeed terrible, and yet God saw something in her heart that He was drawn to. Why would God include her in the family line of His Son if He hadn't somehow looked beyond the awful deeds described in the book of Genesis and seen a hunger, a desperation?

That is the spirit of the Tamar church I am finding in our country and all across the world. It is awesome because it speaks of a hope and a future for our nations. Christians are refusing to lie down and die accepting the status quo. People are refusing just to carry on with the religious Sunday club that is all stimulation and no impartation.

Onan leaders

Five years ago I set out to deliberately impregnate my home church with our future. Yet to some in our church, the child that I deliberately wanted to seed – the child of our future, was an unwanted child. As I began to sow seed and to build, I began to get visits from 'Onan leaders'. Sometimes they would write to me, but usually they would come and see me, sometimes several at a time, and the discussion would go something like this.

'We are not really happy with the things you are saying. Like when you said such and such on Sunday. Have you thought about the implications of that?'

'Yes.'

'But you know if we do *that* as a church, it will mean that we will have to stop doing *this* and give more attention to *that*. Brother Smith, who after all has been running *this* ministry for ten years, was very upset when you said that *this* area needed to change. It sounds like you are planning to make some changes?'

'Absolutely.'

'We don't mind you inspiring us about the vision, but don't get carried away and start changing everything. Let's remember this church's heritage. If we did what you're suggesting there would be chaos.'

In reality we were a comfortable, white middle-class church. I wanted to sow seed into people that would almost certainly endanger that 'comfort'. I wanted to empower people who weren't aware of the history of our church and didn't care about being comfortable.

In the Genesis account Onan said to himself, 'If Tamar has a child by me, I will lose all the firstborn rights that I inherited when my brother died.' As the second son he had become the heir to his father's estate when his older brother had died. If however, Onan made Tamar pregnant and she gave birth to a son, he would forfeit his rights to the child. Sadly, the Onan mentality in the church also says, 'I don't want to help seed anyone else's future if that future will disenfranchise me.'

Onan's message can also take the form of: 'Look, we love the vision you have, we just don't like the way you're going about it.' If the Onans in your church persist it can wear you down. But what if one of them is a key leader in your team, or is a big giver of finance to the church? Then it is very easy to become intimidated. As a leader you have to be aware of, and prepared for, the implications of continuing to preach to the Tamars who are desperate for your input, as you risk completely losing the Onans who may contribute to the life of the church in an important way. Potentially you stand to lose some influential and key people. But this is part of crossing over. This is the risk you take when you decide that only fulfilling the vision God has given you will do. Persist in pursuing what God has told you to do and be aware of the fact that the wrath of Onan will inevitably become apparent long before you see the effects of the seeds you have sown into people's lives. The offspring that will come from Tamar could be weeks, months or even years away. That is why so many leaders quit, because the pressure of Onan tends to be immediate and the rewards of Tamar, longer term.

Before long however, Tamar people began to approach me quietly saying things like, 'Paul, after your message on Sunday I couldn't sleep all week. God has spoken to me and began to open up the possibility of how my life could make a difference in this city and this church. I had a dream about starting a ministry in this church.' People came to me with ideas about reaching the working girls in the red light district; about taking food and clothing to the poor in the city; about reaching people who were going to abort their babies; about reaching the drug users in the city. The seed that was being flung out was making people pregnant with purpose!

The real challenge as a leader comes when you realize that these people, once made pregnant, are not going to go away. They grow in number and you realize that however intimidated you are by the Onans, their days are numbered. If you keep on sowing the seed God has given you, eventually the Tamars will overwhelm the Onans numerically. The ratio will begin to change as you prepare for crossing over. The Onans will tend to become more entrenched in their positions and the gulf will widen.

'Pregnant' churches

I believe our churches should be places of conception. I believe they should be places that contain so much seed that you simply can't help becoming pregnant. If all our churches were imbued with such an expectancy and the possibility for empowerment, every week ordinary people would leave contemplating amazing ideas. Ordinary people doing ordinary things would start to believe that they were capable of extraordinary ministries. These ordinary people who no one ever believed in enough to invest some seed in, will begin doing those amazing things and you will see miracles taking place.

I remember getting multiple reports from the departments of our church that we were in chaos. Our church went into pandemonium for about twelve months. All my training said that the church should be an orderly place, controlled, together, sequential. All of my training was at odds with what was actually happening in the church. At one point I actually stood up in front of the church and told them that I, their leader, had totally lost the plot! I said, 'I am not in control of this church. I have not been in control now for quite some time, in case you hadn't noticed. I don't know what's going on. I do not know what a lot of the people in the church are doing. I don't know the people who are welcoming me to my own church on a Sunday morning. I don't know half the people in the choir. But, I want you to know that it's OK, God's cool with it, because I sense in my heart that He has been waiting a long time for me to get out of control. God has been waiting for me to get on the coat tails of what He has been doing and stop insisting that if I am not in control of everything it can't be decent and orderly.'

According to Genesis 1, God started with chaos. He's not afraid of it. In fact, the leading edge of most major ventures for God tend to look like chaos. It's not always clean, it's not tidy, we are not always sure what it will produce, but let's not be afraid of that. For twenty-five years we had a church so ordered, so together, so well governed, that nothing happened that we didn't know about within hours. I just knew that God couldn't wait to mess our church up. We were in control, but He needed to be in control.

Our church used to be predominantly stimulation with small doses of impartation. It was easy to tell. As I commented earlier on in this book, just the stuff left lying around on the floor during our services taught me that we were not reaching the lost. We were really comfortable with each other. But once we started our bus ministry and not only invited, but actually brought hundreds of the needy of our city to church each week, people started sitting in the meetings holding on to all their stuff! I could see that something was happening, our cozy routines were being messed up! It was forcing us to be different in ways we never thought we would have to be. We liked the Gospel very much when it is just theology. But it was a different story when it became a reality.

All of us must take hold of the responsibility to sow the seed that God has given us – not just leaders. I firmly believe that God will call us to account one day for every seed He has ever thrown in our direction and will want to know what we did with it. Every seed God gives has potential. If we deliberately waste it, then potential has been lost. For everything we didn't do or say that we should have done or said, there will be a reckoning. For everything that we didn't run with for fear of intimidation, there will be a day of reckoning. For every ministry we should have launched, for every empowerment we should have given, I believe God will want an answer. How will we respond to Him? Seed-spilling is a big issue to God. Let us all be determined to sow all that we have, fulfilling our destinies in Christ, and helping as many others as possible to reach theirs.

PART 3

'Crossing Over' People

Chapter 6

Where Are
God's Bravehearts?

Hebrews 11:32–34

In the next three chapters I want to talk about some of the qualities of people who make a decision to cross over into their God-given destinies. What do these people look like? Is there anything about them that sets them apart from the crowd? I hope that you will draw personal encouragement from the following pages and make a decision, if you haven't done so already, to cross over and take hold of absolutely everything that God has for you.

In the closing verses of Hebrews chapter 11, the writer, having spoken about many great heroes of the faith, quickly mentions a few others that he hasn't spoken about in detail. It's like he is running out of time and simply can't finish his writing without mentioning just a few more. He mentions the names of '... *Gideon, Barak, Samson, Jephthah, David, Samuel and the prophets ...'* – people who accomplished phenomenal things for God and changed the face of history. They *wrote* history and yet the writer of Hebrews barely skims over them – even though many of them conquered whole kingdoms for the purposes of God!

'Gaining' the promises of God

Then there comes an important statement. Verse 33 says that these heroes of the faith, '... *administered justice, and gained what was promised* ... ' Notice that they had to *gain* what was promised to them by the Lord. The Bible doesn't say that they *received* it, but they *gained* it. Some Christians never take hold of all that God has for them because they are passively waiting to receive it. It will not come if you are just waiting to receive it. Some promises of God have to be gained. On the whole, Christians are entirely too passive and far too 'British', laid back, and pedestrian about things that are to do with their very lives and destinies.

Are there things that you are believing God will do in your life, or your ministry, or your church? They are not going to come and knock at your front door. The heroes of the faith gained what was promised. You have got to fight for your promises. Sometimes you have got to fight for your health; fight for your household to come to Christ; fight for a financial breakthrough; fight for a circumstantial breakthrough. Whatever the specifics of your situation, it is time to gain what is promised to you.

The peace that we currently have in Britain was gained by two world wars. Those of us who were born in the post-war era and didn't live through the war often can't fully relate to that. Nevertheless, much blood was shed in order to gain the peace we now enjoy. If people who did not know Christ would shed their blood for the peace of a nation – for children yet to be born – then that should stir something inside all of us that refuses to live another day under the oppression of our enemy, the devil. So many Christians are needlessly putting up with so much 'stuff' that the enemy slings at them. Some are praying about it and constantly having prayer ministry or counseling, and still nothing changes. If this is you, why don't you try getting really angry about it? Why don't you take your coat off about it? Christ died to buy your freedom. When you gave your life to Him that promise came into effect for your life. It is promised to you. Get aggressive about it and *gain* what God has promised you.

The problem comes when you don't want what God has promised you badly enough. If you don't want it badly enough, then God won't give it to you. *If you want to have something that you've never had, then you've got to do something you've never done.* There is nothing more foolish than doing the same thing over and over again and expecting a different outcome. You've got to come to each situation in life wanting to grab whatever God has promised you. That is why in this chapter I am asking the question, 'Where are God's Bravehearts?'

In order to begin to answer this question, let's look at verse 34 of Hebrews 11. It says of these heroes that their '. . . *weakness was turned to strength* . . . ' In other words, these were people who didn't start out strong. Gideon didn't start strong; Moses didn't; Joseph didn't, Rahab the prostitute didn't. But during the course of their lives they were shaped by God and their weakness was gradually turned into strength. In life it is not how you start that matters, but how you finish. Some reading this will have had an awful start in life. Maybe you were born into a dysfunctional family, or were orphaned at birth? Maybe you were raised in an abusive situation. Maybe you missed out on any opportunity for education? You have a choice. Either you can complain to God about the awful start you had in life, or you can decide to fight for and gain all He has planned for you.

Finishing well

It doesn't matter how bad your start was. Jesus had an awful start. What matters is how you finish. And how you finish is not determined by God, it is determined by your response to what God has planned for your life. Jesus Christ is the Alpha and the Omega, He is God's 'Omega man' – He is a fantastic finisher. On the cross He said the three most important, most powerful words ever spoken in human speech: *'It is finished.'* He didn't say 'I am finished' but 'It is finished.' He was in control of what was happening to Him all along. He bowed out because He had done what He came to do. Jesus is not as concerned about how your life started as He is about how it will finish.

Proof of the importance of finishing well can be seen in the testimonies of Palti, Shaphat and Igal. Who? You might well ask! Palti, Shaphat and Igal were three of the twelve spies sent by Moses to scout the Promised Land. Why is it that we know nothing about them? Because they didn't finish well. How many kids are there running around named Palti? How many Igals do you know? None, because they weren't good finishers. There are plenty of Joshuas and Calebs running around though. People want to be associated with those who finish well.

The heroes of Hebrews 11 are described as being 'mighty in battle'. Mightiness can only be achieved by surviving successive fights and battles. Battles make you stronger. You truly appreciate those things in life that you have had to struggle to attain. As we noted in Chapter 1, the Hebrews 11 list is not one of 'holy' people who were especially righteous, pious or lived perfect lives. They were named for their faith and courage. They had the courage to believe God for outrageous things and He rewarded their courage.

God loves courage

God loves courageous people. Yet, so many people are discouraged. Discouragement has reached epidemic proportions in the Church of God. God will respond to your courage, despite the fact that you've been listening to the discouraging things that people say to you. 'God won't use you until you get that issue in your life sorted out' they say. That's not true. Obviously God can't use you if you are refusing to cooperate with Him, or if you are living in willful, sinful rebellion towards Him. But the heroes of Hebrews 11 didn't all have their lives together, nowhere near. Rahab was a prostitute. She wasn't a prostitute twenty-five years ago before she got saved and so God was now able to use her. No, she was a currently practicing prostitute when God used her and recorded her name in both Hebrews 11 and the genealogy of Jesus Christ. Why was she so esteemed? Because of her courage. She stuck her neck out, she risked her life and her family for the purposes of God, and God said, 'I like that. I don't care if she is a gentile, a heathen and a prostitute. I love her courage.'

Cowardice turns pilgrims into wanderers. That is what happened to Israel in the wilderness. They were cowards. It wasn't God's heart for them to walk around for forty years. God could have taken them into Canaan within two weeks, but because they had no stomach for warfare they condemned themselves to a forty-year diversion. Cowardice will turn your own pilgrimage into an aimless wandering too. Unless you get something of courage working in your heart and soul you will waste a lot of time trying to circumvent every confrontation; you will never stand for anything; you will never fight for anything; you will never get involved in anything that upsets people, or makes people not like you.

Are you living your life like that? Some people have lived their entire lives inside the permissions and approval of others. They live to win the acceptance of others. If you can honestly say to yourself that you don't feel you've lived the life God wants you to live, then something must change now. Stop being a slave to other people's opinions. Don't hesitate to be courageous for God for fear that someone might point a finger of disapproval at you.

For years I lived in that trap myself, until I became sick and tired of what it was doing to me; what it was doing to my wife and children because I was not being myself. God would give me things to say and I wouldn't say them. I didn't say them because I knew there were people who wouldn't approve of me saying those things. I was like that. It gets you knotted up, paranoid and scared of yourself. Thank the Lord that He delivered me from being a slave to opinion! Nowadays I couldn't care less what people say or think about me. I'm just here to say whatever God wants to say through me. I used to be people-centered in my leadership, but now I am God-centered in my leadership. I can no longer dance to the tune people play, which is just as well because some play a different tune every week! Jesus couldn't please everybody. Moses couldn't and he was the meekest man on the face of the earth. If Moses couldn't please everyone, who do we think we are?

God loves to say 'Yes'!

'Religion' has taught us that God is a Person who loves to say '**No**'. Religion has trained us to believe He is inclined to deny and withhold. The fact that we know He is holy and knows what is best for us only seems to add credence to the myth. We think that God might occasionally say

'Yes' to our requests, but that on the whole the answer will be 'No'. Does that sound too far-fetched? Yet this is how many people view God. But God is actually a 'Yes' Person. He delights in saying 'Yes' to the desires of our hearts. He is wanting us to come to Him and ask for things just so He can say 'Yes' to us.

When God spoke to me about starting the bus ministry our church runs, bringing unsaved people in large numbers to the church, I wanted a confirmation from Him before I went public with it. Sometimes you want God to give you a sign, a little nudge to help you get the necessary courage. The very morning I was saying that to God, I was walking my dog along a canal tow path. As I turned the corner on my usual circuit to cut across a school playing field, right there on the ground in front of me was a piece of paper ripped out of a kid's text book, and it had some handwriting on it. The wind was blowing and yet the paper wasn't moving. It was white and in pristine condition. I thought to myself, 'Well I've asked the question so I might as well have a look at this piece of paper. You never know ... 'When I picked it up, I couldn't believe my eyes! At the top of the paper it said, 'Transport is extremely important'. The next line said, 'Because of it, the population has exploded' and it continued, 'Because the population exploded, industry exploded, and because industry exploded employment came to the city of London'. I realized that it was an essay from a kids book about the industrialization of London at the turn of the century. After I read that, God said to me, 'What more do you want? Do you want the dog to talk?' God said that if I got the buses going my church would explode and prosperity would come to the city; people's lives would be blessed and prosperity would come to the people we reached out to.

You may say to me, 'Paul, I stepped out with courage for God, but I got hurt and I crashed and burned.'

Whenever people say that to me, I tell them this little story:

There was once a little Canadian bird that wouldn't fly south for the winter. It decided that this year it was not going to fly south for winter like the rest of those birds, it was going to nestle right where it was in its nest for the winter and not expend all that energy and take that risk. So all the birds went and the little bird waved them off and then nestled into its nest. A few days later the weather took a turn for the worst and became very cold. The little bird started to get a bit bothered and started thinking of all its friends who were probably sunning themselves in Mexico by now. Eventually it decided that it would go south after all. It was a few hours into its flight when the weather got worse still and it rained heavily. The rain turned to ice on its wings. It began to freeze to death. It couldn't continue and eventually it plummeted and crashed into the middle of a barnyard in the countryside. The bird was gasping its last dying breath and wishing it had gone in the first place, when suddenly the barnyard cow came over to it, looked down and did an enormous poop on the bird! The bird thought to itself, 'This is absolutely ridiculous. I'm dying. It's my final moment on this earth, and now to add insult to injury this cow has pooped on me.' It lay back ready to die, but after a while began to realize that the poop was kind of warming! It began to get the feeling back in its wings and its body began to thaw out. Suddenly the bird realized, 'I'm not going to die, I'm going to live!' It began to get excited and its wings started to flap and it began to sing and chirp. However, all his chirping and singing alerted the attention of the barnyard cat. The cat sauntered over, picked up the little bird and began to scrape the poop off him. And when the cat had cleaned the little bird up . . . he ate him! End of story!

There are three morals to this story:

1. Not everyone who poops on you is your enemy.

2. Not everyone who scrapes it off is your friend.

3. If some one poops on you, keep your mouth shut!

Some Christians are still complaining to God about times when they were pooped on by others. For some it may be an event that took place years ago and they still haven't gotten over it. If this is you, it is time to get up, get over it, and head for the place where you were going when you got pooped on. Don't let people or circumstances hold you down. Your destiny is too precious. God is looking for His Bravehearts –those who refuse to be put in a box or squeezed into a mould.

Today God is saying to you, 'You have no idea what is inside your life; what you could achieve; what I have planned for your life.' What you do with this gift of God is up to you. Get up from the place of discouragement and move into what God has destined you to do.

You and I have been put on the face of the earth today to be God's Bravehearts. Here in this dark period of history we will see some of the greatest heroes, heroines, martyrs and saviors emerge who ever walked the face of the earth. They will be warlike, confrontational, unreasonable people who refuse to compromise.

In those last verses of Hebrews 11, the 'other' heroes of the faith that are hurriedly mentioned are mainly the judges of Israel – Gideon, Barak, Samson, Jephthah. God raised up these judges because His people were being constantly oppressed, raided over and over again by warring nations. They were just ordinary people, but there came a day when something snapped in each one of them and they were no longer prepared to put up with the status quo. Often the miracle you need from God is not one that happens in your circumstances, but one that happens in your heart. Take courage! Be one of God's Bravehearts.

Chapter 7

The Power to Become

John 1:11–13

The concept of 'entering the promised land' spiritually is to do with becoming all that you are destined to be in Christ. In this chapter I want to show that every one of us has *the power to become* what God has planned for us to become. We are talking about *becoming* and not *getting*. I am not talking about an 'If you confess it then you can have it' kind of attitude, but a very real power that abides inside every believer by the Holy Spirit. You may not feel it. It entered your life quietly, by stealth, but don't kid yourself that it is not there.

I want to see churches built in our nation that help people realize that when they are saved, God invests an awesome power inside them. It is a unique power unlike anything else in the universe – the power to become a child of God – a son or daughter of the Father.

When you are born, you are born with the all the necessary biological functions and genetic information to grow physically. But you don't immediately realize that you have the power, the ability to become all that you have the potential to become – to be all your parents dream and hope you'll be. In order to do that, you have to undergo some training, shaping and discipline. You have to be guided and corrected. Some of us have to be knocked into shape! But the Bible teaches that when we are saved, God puts a kind of divine 'want to' in our spirits.

It doesn't matter how you got saved, whether you wept, fell over or whatever. Regardless of the time, place or circumstances, as soon as you gave your life to Jesus you received the 'power to become'.

> ' . . . to all who received him, to those who believed in his name, he gave the right **to become children of God** – children born not of natural descent, nor of human decision or a husband's will, but born of God.'
>
> (John 1:12–13)

Those who have received Jesus have the power to become the children of God. The word 'become' means 'to cause to be'. It means the power to be assembled. God gave you the power to be assembled in the way He wanted. Imagine buying a flat-pack wardrobe, taking it up to the bedroom, dropping the pack on the floor and saying, 'Go ahead and be a wardrobe.' It sounds absurd, but that is exactly what you have just read in the scripture above. Often the Church has been guilty of spreading a myth. The myth is that being saved isn't enough in itself. We don't believe it can be that simple, and so we load people down with 'stuff' to compensate for what God 'cannot' do. And just in case you're not convinced you are saved, the Church works hard to persuade you, convince you, inspire you, cajole you – just in case you don't believe anything has really happened.

Self-assembly

We need to get back to basics. Read Acts 2. See what took place in the early Church; look at what the first generation of believers were like, how they behaved. Now take a look at what we have made church today. Look at all the stuff we have added. What's left when you take all these additives away? What's left is the model that we should have seen and understood in the first place – a simple life of discipleship infused with the power of God.

What often meets us as believers is a lot of stuff that we don't need. We all need to come to the place of understanding that Christ is all-sufficient for us. We have made ourselves dependent on so many things. We rely upon things and people, and we have made them our gods, not allowing God to be God. We are quicker to talk to another person about a problem than we are to talk to God about it. We are quicker to ask someone to lay hands on us than to ask for God's hand to come on our life.

God's power within you means that you have the power to self-assemble yourself from within. You don't need to load yourself down with more counseling sessions or stand in another prayer line for it to happen. You don't need another visit from someone or a personal prophecy. God is saying all you need to do is to get into the flow of the Holy Spirit's power that is inside you – the power to become everything you dreamed of, or wanted to become.

Not only did God put within you the power to become when you were saved, He also gave you the desire to *want to become*. James 4:5 in the Amplified Bible says,

> *'The Spirit Whom he has caused to dwell in us yearns over us ... with a jealous love.'*

And King David put it this way in Psalm 42:1,

> *'As the deer pants for streams of water,*
> *so my soul* [inner self] *pants for you, O God.'*

⚔'Panting' for God

David had a panting soul. I want to see churches built that are full of 'panting' people – not churches full of people who have to be spoon-fed – churches that are pregnant with a divine 'want to'. When you were saved, God gave you a 'becoming gene' and a 'panting gene'. In one of his Psalms David protests, 'When can I go and meet with God?' It's like he was counting the moments and the hours until he could get away from his kingly responsibilities and just be in the presence of God. In Psalm 84:2 he continues,

> *'My soul yearns, even faints,*
> *for the courts of the LORD;*
> *my heart and my flesh cry out*
> *for the living God.'*

He wanted to get away from the 'stuff' of his life and just be himself – to become a little more 'assembled' in the presence of His Maker.

Inside everyone, just like David, the divine 'want to' is crying out – crying out for more of God's presence in your life, crying out to become all He destined you to be. You may be tired, but inside you want to run and jump; you may be broke, but inside you want to give; you may be sad, but inside you have a joy that is unspeakable and full of glory; you may be shy, but inside there is a shout; you may feel embarrassed, but inside there is a lion trying to get out. You may not think you have a great prayer life, yet there is something inside you that constantly wants to pray and commune and fellowship and walk with God. You may not be too good at reading your Bible, but there is something inside you that just wants to devour the Word of God all the time.

You may say, 'Hang on, I don't feel any of this …'

That is your problem. You are waiting until you *feel it*. If you wait until you feel it, whatever it is, it will be too late. Stop waiting until you feel something in your emotional realm. We have made our Christianity far too touchy-feely. We need to believe what God has said about us in His Word, connect with it in our spirit and live it out in reality.

It is wonderful to be around people who are flowing in the power to become. They don't depend on external things to become a son of God. They are not waiting for the next meeting. They are not depending on the next opportunity for laying on of hands or rolling in the aisles. They are in touch with a divine power to become. Isaiah 53:2 says of Jesus that He was *'like a root out of dry ground'* – in other words He wasn't dependent on external things for the fruitfulness of His life. It didn't matter to Jesus whether He was being persecuted or praised; whether the crowd took up stones to throw at Him or bowed down to worship Him. No such external circumstances fazed Him because He knew the power inside Him. He relied upon the power of the Spirit within Him to enable Him to do all He needed to do.

Jesus didn't feel discouraged when the officials came to arrest Him in the garden of Gethsemane. Inside Himself He was immune. He knew what God had destined Him to be, and what He had to do. Inside Him was the divine power to be all that God intended His Son to become in His thirty-three years on the earth.

Chilling out

When you connect with the power inside of you to become all that God destined you to be, living the Christian life no longer seems such hard work. You begin to flow in the power of the Holy Spirit and life seems easy. Even when you face challenges, problems and difficulties you won't be fazed by them because of the peace and power within. God is saying, 'Church, chill out!' Jesus did a complete work for us on the cross. He did the hard part for us, and it is because of all He did that we who believe in Him now have His power resident within us. All we need to do is to trust Him and ask Him to help us connect with the power of the Holy Spirit that He put within us. Some of us need to quit worrying so much. It's nor our responsibility to run the universe!

I have realized that over the last few years of my journey with God, I have become so chilled out that it's a bit scary! I am not bothered about stuff anymore that used to really occupy my leadership and my life. When people come and people go in the life of the church it doesn't worry me like it used to. That is part of my discovery – I have to chill out, I am not the Lord of our church. I didn't die for the people who come to our church; I didn't shed my blood for them; I am not the good shepherd, I can't keep everyone happy. I chilled out and it changed my life. I didn't go to a seminar to get a better theology, I just realized that if I kept living the way I was I would have a heart attack or get burned out and quit the ministry. Instead God has helped me to connect with the power of His Spirit within me – to connect with my 'becomer' and stop striving; to flow with His peace and His presence. Today we have a growing church that seeks to reach millions around the world through our TV ministry. We have a huge budget and massive financial challenges. There are bills to pay and some borrowings to clear, but we are doing what God has called us to do. So, if I don't chill out about all of that I will be a nervous wreck and a poor leader.

Learning to flow

The more we walk with Jesus and spend time with Him the more we will become like Him. But it needn't be stressful or pressured. We need to allow God to be God, and ourselves to be ourselves. God doesn't think He's you and you don't need to try to be Him. These are the best days of our lives, and if we spend the best days of our lives all tense and screwed up, then we have missed the whole point. Have you ever had the feeling, 'I think I am missing the plot here'? When you are in the flow of the Spirit you don't miss anything. When you are in the flow, everything you dreamed of or imagined is somewhere in that flow. It maybe a bit further down stream, but don't get out of the flow and go on dry land to try and find it. Stay close to Jesus and keeping flowing with the Holy Spirit. If you stay in the flow you will eventually come to it. Just stay inside the flow. Seek first the Kingdom of God and all these things will be given to you.

As we learn to live in the flow individually then we will learn to flow together as a community of believers. Look at the description of the early Church found at the end of Acts chapter 2:

> 'They devoted themselves to the apostles' teaching and to the fellowship, to the breaking of bread and to prayer. Everyone was filled with awe, and many wonders and miraculous signs were done by the apostles. All the believers were together and had everything in common. Selling their possessions and goods, they gave to anyone as he had need. Every day they continued to meet together in the temple courts. They broke bread in their homes and ate together with glad and sincere hearts, praising God and enjoying the favor of all the people. And the Lord added to their number daily those who were being saved.'
>
> (Acts 2:42–47)

If you were God, wouldn't you want to send people to a church like that? If we learn to live in the flow of the Holy Spirit, then together we can have church that is like that. Two thousand years later we seem to have really messed up. We need to return to God's original intentions for us. Something strange has happened to our liberty. Something sinister has happened to the purity of the flow of the life of Christ in the Church. Even as we read this passage in Acts we are found wanting. This passage drops a plumb-line into the Church and it begs some major questions. Today we need churches that are like this community of early believers. We don't need more church *members* to be successful, but we do need more hungry, seeking believers. I don't see church membership in the Bible anyway. To be a 'member' of the early New Testament church involved a supernatural initiative. God 'plugged' people into the Church. They were supernaturally 'added' by Him according to His will and purpose.

In that sense, because you didn't 'join' the Church but were 'added', then you can't leave! If Christians really grasped this and committed themselves to the churches where God 'added' them when they were saved, then it would mean that less would jump from church to church when they felt like it. Christians wouldn't flit from place to place because 'the worship is better' or 'the preaching is better' or 'the people are nicer', but would remain committed to ' ... *the apostles' teaching and to the fellowship* ... '. As a leader reading this, it is your responsibility to ensure that you build a strong God-centered, people-empowering church.

Success comes from staying with where God has put you. Many people have found that out to their cost. If you play fast and loose with church you are going to have a hard time. Stay where God has added you. Avoid becoming a spiritual gypsy. Avoid 'goose bump' Christianity.

You can't build a solid church with constantly moving Christians, just as you can't build a building with moving bricks. It's challenging. It is turning on its head things that we have been told for many years that are simply not biblical.

When we are flowing together in God's purposes then we naturally begin to get into each other's lives. We become aware of each other's needs and problems and we express commitment by helping one another. Our primary commitment is always to Christ and His kingdom because that is what gives us our purpose, and purpose helps us to keep flowing together.

So the power to become can now apply to a whole body of believers. At our church we are learning to flow together more all the time. The purpose which keeps us flowing together is to extend God's kingdom and to reach our city and world. Our aim is to be a purpose-driven church. I want us to be like a moving train. We won't slow down for people to casually hop on; we are going to keep moving and you can catch us if you can! That's how Jesus operated. He wasn't going to hang around trying to convince people to follow Him, He just kept moving, flowing with God's purposes and those who couldn't flow with Him probably weren't meant to.

I had a friend in the USA who was in prison and who had formerly carried out a number of bank robberies. He told me that he used to go and ask advice on how to do it from some of the old crooks in prison. They told him, 'You need three people to do a bank job. Someone who is good at handling the crowd of people, someone who is good with a gun, and a good driver. The three of you have got to be able to work together well and everything needs to flow.'

He told me that he once did a bank job where they got the flow all wrong. Two of them were in the bank, but the guy who was handling the crowd was getting it all wrong. He was a lunatic and was scaring everybody to death, causing pandemonium instead of calmly taking control. When they came running out with the money they found that the driver had gotten out of the car and gone into a shop because he thought he had plenty of time! So they were left standing outside the bank holding the bulging bags of cash!

I have been to plenty of churches like that. The people haven't learned to flow together. There are people in the wrong roles, doing things that they aren't gifted to do. There's no sense of direction or purpose holding them together and taking them forward. Understanding the flow can save a lot of heartache and wasted effort.

We need to decide individually that we are going to connect with the power God has put within us to become like His Son, Jesus, and we need to connect with one another, just as the early Church did, and learn to flow together in the purposes of God. When we do that we will truly see the power of God in our nation and His Kingdom begin to be extended at a faster rate than we have ever witnessed before.

Chapter 8

The Incorruptible Seed

1 Peter 1:18–23

'... you were not redeemed with corruptible things, like silver or gold, from your aimless conduct received by tradition from your fathers, but with the precious blood of Christ, as of a lamb without blemish and without spot ... having been born again, not of corruptible seed but incorruptible, through the word of God which lives and abides forever ...'   (1 Peter 1:18–23, NKJV)

Here Peter makes an amazing statement. He says that when we were saved, we were saved by and through the *incorruptible seed* of the living and enduring Word of God. When we were saved, we were given an incorruptible seed. It's another way of saying that God invested in us the power to become.

What are seeds? Seeds are miracle capsules. Seeds are the tomorrow that you would like, but you must plant them today. Seeds represent the life that you want. Seeds are your future. Now here is the incredible thing about seeds: no seed in the world is incorruptible. Every seed can be damaged. Every seed can be affected. Every seed can be diseased. Every seed can be disturbed or genetically modified. No seed in the world is immune from corruption or from being tampered with. But when you and I got saved the Bible says that God gave us an *incorruptible* seed. The incorruptible seed was dropped into your life the moment you came to Christ.

It does not matter when, how or why you were saved. People sometimes compare their own salvation experience to that of others and are disappointed if theirs doesn't sound as exciting or dramatic. Some people can describe their encounter with God in glorious Technicolor. They can quote the date, describe the atmosphere, tell you how they felt. Others heard and felt nothing, but just quietly knew God had met with them. When you hear of dramatic conversions you can be tempted to think, 'Wow! That was radical; they were really saved.' But hang on ... what other kind of conversion is there? The Bible only knows 'really radically saved'. You can't be 95% saved. You are either saved or you are lost. Once you were in the kingdom of darkness and now you are in the kingdom of light. What could be more radical than that?

When you were saved you were given all the power you needed at that moment of conversion. The Bible says that you were given all the power you needed for life and for godliness. How did God do that? He gave you His incorruptible seed.

Growing up in God

Here Peter is beginning to teach something to the Church that some of us still haven't understood. He said that when you were born again, you were not born again of corruptible seed, you were born with an incorruptible seed – in other words, the stuff that only God deals in. If you are born again you've already got this incorruptible seed in you. Stop trying to find it, you've got it. You can't buy it or borrow it, you got it when you were saved. We have made our Christianity in the twenty-first century all touch-feely. We want to feel things, to have a buzz instead of just believing what the Bible says is true about us. Is God any less present in our lives when we don't feel Him? Is there less power or anointing in our lives when we don't feel it?

We are in danger of believing that we engage God with our five senses only. Peter is teaching us these truths so that we will become grounded in our faith and not be pulled this way and that by our feelings. Peter is not giving us milk! This is heavy stuff. It is intended to separate you from your childish ways in the faith. It will cause you to grow up. This teaching will stop you borrowing other people to become a crutch for you. It will stop you asking God to do something that He can never do for you, because He has already done everything for you. You are never going to be more saved than you already are. The Bible says get on with your faith and work it out. Work out your salvation with fear and trembling (Philippians 2:12).

Incorruptible means everlasting, it means imperishable, it means cannot be bribed and cannot be tempted. Do you know that there is a part of you that cannot be tempted? Do you know that there is a part of your make up as a believer that is immune from temptation? It is the incorruptible seed part of you. If you will live from this part of you instead of living from your mind and living from your emotions, you will find that an immunity to temptation kicks in to your life. I hear Christians saying all the time, 'I struggle with temptation, I struggle with awful thoughts and passions and desires I shouldn't have.' Where are you living from? If you live an emotion-based Christianity you are a sitting duck for the devil. He will plague your emotions. James wrote that when we are tempted it is because we are dragged away, enticed by our own carnal desires (James 1:13–15).

But there are no carnal desires in the incorruptible part of us. It is incorruptible; by its very nature it cannot be tempted. How can you tempt something that's incorruptible? If it could be tempted it would immediately become corruptible.

If you live your Christianity from your un-renewed mind, then you are a statistic waiting to happen. The devil knows how to play mind games. He will plague you in your mind and he will sow thoughts persistently until they become a stronghold in your mind. Once a stronghold has been established in your mind it can be turned into a habit. And once you have a habit then it's time to join the prayer line again ... This is the vicious circle of a Christianity robbed of its power. Some people actually don't need counseling or prayer or deliverance – they just need to grow up, realize that they are saved and live saved!

Many people do have genuine problems and need help to find a solution, but I suspect that there are many more stuck on the 'book, tape and conference bandwagon'. They think that the answer to their problems in life will be found in the next tape they listen to, or the next book they read, or the next special meeting they go to. And worse still, there are plenty of people who are cashing in on that demand by providing the material. If Christians woke up and truly realized how saved they were, many of these people would be going out to look for a proper job! In you is the divine seed, the incorruptible seed of the Word of God. And if you live from this part of you, all your problems will suddenly come into perspective.

Jesus spoke from the incorruptible seed of the Word

When the devil came to tempt Jesus in the desert, he tried to find a corruptible part of Him. He knew Jesus must be really hungry, so he tried to tempt Him to satisfy His appetite. He tried to give Jesus an easy way out of the hard trials He had ahead by tempting Him to bow down and worship him. He tried everything to appeal to something in Jesus that temptation could latch itself onto. But temptation will not be successful if it finds nothing in your life to attach itself to. What did Jesus do? He answered from the incorruptible seed of the Word inside Him. He answered three times, '*It is written ... it is written ... it is written ...*' (Matthew 4:1–11). Jesus was living on the Word of God, in fact He was that same 'Word made flesh' (John 1:1). Consequently, He answered from that Word. What we often try to do is to get smart with the devil and debate with him. We try to make a deal with him; we try to manipulate him; we try to let him become a squatter in the back bedroom of our house, instead of responding from the Word and rendering him powerless.

The devil doesn't like people talking like this, because when believers begin to see just how God has empowered them, they begin rising up – an army of powerful, God-centered, purpose-driven believers, scary to the devil. Many Christians read the Word and think, 'It can't be referring to me.' But always remember, these promises are not just for leaders or super-Christians, they are for all of us.

When the devil comes to tempt you, it is no good saying to him, 'Well, this is what I *think* is written.' If that's where you are at you are in danger. That is what Eve tried to do. The devil asked her, 'Did God really say ...?' because he knew she wasn't around when God had said it to Adam. She was in possession of second-hand information. If you don't know what God really said, then the devil is going to keep on asking you stuff that he knows you don't know. That is why we have got to get the Word of God into our bones. When we do, it feeds and fills us out. It's no good saying, 'This is what my pastor said is written ...' You have to know for yourself.

Some people are living from their mind, their soul, or even just from experience to experience, from situation to situation. I want to see churches built where every believer is taught to live from the incorruptible part of them – where they individually live from the Word.

The only other person besides Jesus who ever had an incorruptible walk with God was Adam, before he fell. Adam lived from a part of him that was special, but no more special than that which God has put inside every believer. Adam woke up into a created order and walked with God from this incorruptible center until one day he let his guard down and fell. After he sinned and fell, he reacted uncharacteristically by hiding himself from God. Anything that has been corrupted, infected, compromised, abused, from that moment onwards lives in reaction. If you have had your trust betrayed, from that moment on you become a bit more guarded. If you have been lied to, you tend to become a bit more suspicious. But this incorruptible seed has never been tainted, it doesn't react out of the pain of past hurts; it doesn't respond to things irrationally. If we live from this part of us, then we will enjoy a much more balanced, peaceful life – free from sudden swings of emotion and impulsiveness.

If many Christians didn't have problems, they would backslide because they wouldn't pray or read their Bible. Why is it that when people are doing well, they don't come to church, or pray or read the Bible? But if they have some sudden crisis in their life, 'boom', they are in church like a shot. Why is it that people play fast and loose with God, then when they lose their job – which was their real security – they are in church in the prayer line weeping? We shouldn't need to have a problem to

draw us to God. Adam didn't walk with God in the cool
of the day and discuss his problems. Adam didn't cleave
to God because things were going on that he couldn't
control. Adam just loved God for who He was. He walked
with Him and served Him. Adam's life was incorruptible
and the devil knew he had to find some chink in his
armor in order to get to him – something that would
appeal to his mind, to his soul. There was no other way
in. Where is God's headquarters inside you? Is it in the
incorruptible part of your life that God has put inside
you?

Every human being since Adam has been born into
corruption. Every child is born with an innate resistance
towards God that has to be overcome by salvation, and
must be followed by a full surrender of our lives to Christ
as Lord so that the pattern of corruption is broken.
Salvation is our deliverance from the negative 'reaction'
we had towards God as a result of living under the
contamination of the Fall.

The incorruptible seed cannot be dulled by alcohol, it
cannot be clouded by drugs. There is no knife that can
cut it out. There is no anesthetic that can dull its effect.
There is no relationship that can make it go away. There
is nothing you can do that can change the fact that it has
entered your life and will remain there forever and ever.

The incorruptible part of you is immune to the inter-
ference of life's circumstances. That which is incorruptible
cannot be tired, or exhausted, or weary, or depressed. It is
immortal, invincible and awesome. There is no tiredness,
no burn out in this part of your life. God invested His
incorruptible seed in each one of us the same. Do you
know what that means? It means that Billy Graham is no
more saved than you. It means that the great apostle Peter
was no more saved than you. It means that the great
apostle Paul who wrote a third of the New Testament, the
greatest apostle of all time, was no more saved than you.

He got the same deal. The same incorruptible seed that saved him, is the same incorruptible seed that saved you.

If you live from this part of you, then you will know what you should and shouldn't be doing with your life. If you live from this part of you, the devil is powerless to destroy you. Learn to live from this incorruptible part of your life and you will enjoy living in your 'promised land'.

Part 4

'Crossing Over' Churches

Chapter 9

They Devoted Themselves

Acts 2:42–47

We have now examined some of the qualities needed by the leaders of churches wanting to 'cross over' and some of the characteristics essential for the individual Christians in those churches. In the next two chapters I turn to our corporate experience and will examine two specific facets of crossing over churches. The first concerning what they are like – the makeup of their DNA – and the second, concerning what they can do to help and bless others. In this chapter I will expand upon the theme of Acts chapter 2 where we read about the early Church believers and how they conducted themselves.

Words can mean different things. Some years ago when I first began to travel to the States, I remember staying with a Pastor and his wife in St. Louis. We had stayed there for a week and as we were leaving I said to the pastors wife, 'You know, you are the most homely person I've ever stayed with.' She just froze and didn't respond. I thought, 'Poor soul, she's not receiving this. She must have a terrible self-image.' So I just kept pressing the issue. I said, 'You are very homely, so homely.' No one told me that what I was saying was,

'You are so ugly – the most ugly person I have ever stayed with in my life,' and I was just laboring this thing! Then in the same church at the Sunday morning meeting I said to everyone, 'That was a great time in God's presence, now go home and enjoy your Sunday joint.' It's such a familiar saying in England, meaning to go home and have a roast dinner. I had no idea I was encouraging the church to go home and smoke marijuana! The young people loved it! I remember at another church, I was struck coming into the car park by how untidy and messy it was, so I mentioned to the congregation 'You know, I've noticed there are a lot of fags in the car park, so if you could pick them up on your way out ... '! Of course they are just cigarette butts in England but in the USA it is a derogatory term for a homosexual. Anyway, I've never been invited back to any of those churches!

In the same way we can read the words of the Bible over and over again and still think that they mean something else. We don't spot the obvious. We miss the real meaning. We can read them and interpret them to mean something completely different than was originally intended. In this chapter I want us to examine the first three words ever written about the early Church. If we can understand and apply them then we will uncover one of the devil's best kept secrets and find one of the missing keys to the health, vitality and growth of the early Church.

Three words ...

These three words are so un-dynamic that you would not want to be caught trying to preach them if your aim was to excite and inspire people. These words are not part of the dynamic of the miracles, signs and wonders that come later in this passage, but these three words are the bedrock from which the growth and the advance of the kingdom sprang. They released the supernatural and as a result many people were added to the Church.

What are these three overlooked, underestimated, undervalued words? *'They devoted themselves'.*

> *'They devoted themselves to the apostles' teaching, and to the fellowship, to the breaking of bread and to prayer. Everyone was filled with awe, and many wonders and miraculous signs were done by the apostles. All the believers were together and had everything in common. Selling their possessions and goods they gave to anyone as they had need. Every day they continued to meet together with glad and sincere hearts, praising God and enjoying the favor of all the people.'* (Acts 2:42–47)

There was a great spontaneity within this community. They sold their possessions in order to give to anyone who lacked in any way. There was a devotion to one another, to help and to care. They didn't have a structured program. And notice what God got to do. Because the believers were committed to supplying one another's needs, it released God to just do what God does best: *'... and the Lord added to their number daily those who were being saved.'* The early Church thrived on personal, individual, devotion to God. The energy and the initiative for living the Christian life that existed in the early Church is our heritage. It is how the Church began, how it developed and thrived, and it is the model that we should be looking to emulate.

We have much to learn from this. There is much in the early Church that we should be copying today. The energy, the life, the initiative, the motivation for living the Christian life, sprang from within the people. It didn't come from having the right programs, or a great worship band, or great preaching. The life of the early

Church sprang from the bottom up, not from the top down.

Establishing the flow

This came home to me again recently, talking to an ex-Baptist Pastor in our country, who for twenty years had been in ministry in the same church. He and his wife had a nervous breakdown and finished up ill and on medication. I was speaking to him and was shocked to hear that he was now a pub landlord. I asked him, 'What happened?' He said, 'I just got so worn out, trying to get the people to commit, to serve, to give, and to get behind anything I said to them.' He said, 'We got so discouraged.' However, he told me that he loved being a pub landlord. I asked him why and he said, 'Well, my drinkers are devoted all by themselves. I've never had to send out a flyer, reminding them to come back. I've never had to phone them up to say, "You will come tonight won't you?" I've never had to sit wondering if anyone will come to my pub tonight, in fact I have to ring a bell at the end of the night to tell them it's time to go home. I have to practically push them out the door. I never ever saw that in the church in twenty years of ministry.' He was telling me something, without telling me something. He was saying something to me that was strengthening my own convictions about the true nature of the church. It is the same when you set out to build a church as it is with anything in life that you want to build to be a success – a business, a marriage, a building – everything successful in life is established around a flow.

No one builds a building and then says, 'OK, what shall we use this for?' There is a discussion that takes place behind the scenes. How people will 'flow' through the

building is a critical phase of the planning and development. Where will the entrances and exits be? Even which
way the doors will open is thought through. Understanding flow is critical to development. Misunderstanding
flow, or assuming that flow is not important can be very
dangerous.

We have to get back to the Bible definition of 'church'
if we want to grow vibrant, relevant churches. A devotion similar to that of the early Church is the greatest gift
that a believer can hand to a leader. The early Church
leadership were handed a priceless gift. They didn't need
to worry about their church members showing up at
meetings, or reading their Bibles, or praying, or taking
care of one another's needs, or being committed to small
groups. They were *devoted* to the teaching of the Apostles
and they lived out what they were taught. They loved to
serve one another. They didn't need to be coerced or
persuaded or nagged. They were devoted, all by themselves, and that meant that the leadership was released to
do what leaders do best, which is lead! One of the most
vital ingredients of the early Church which helped it
advance, and which is missing from many modern
churches, was the freedom afforded the leaders. They
were not bogged down by the vast array of tasks that
most of today's leaders are.

If it was possible to take an early Church believer and
drop them in the middle of the Church in the twenty-
first century, I think they would be shocked at what most
pastors and leaders do. I think they would be shocked at
how much time is taken up in our churches persuading,
coercing, convincing, nagging and repeating things that
we shouldn't even need to talk about. Those early
believers were desperate to know what was going on
and how they could be involved. They took the initiative
to be involved, to serve, to plug in to what was happening to advance the kingdom of God. It was springing

from inside them. They had as much desire in them to
see God's kingdom advance as the Apostles did. It was
not a case of, 'Well, if the Apostles inspire us we might be
interested in getting involved. It depends how well they
sell it to us ...'

The leaders of the early Church were delivered from
the stuff that causes burn outs and destroys many pastors
and leaders. They were free from compensatory leadership – leadership that compensates for that which the
church isn't doing; the things that you have to do
yourself otherwise they won't get done at all. Much
modern leadership is born out of reacting and compen-
sating, but the early Church leaders were released from
all of that because the believers devoted themselves.

It's follow-up, but not as we know it

A while ago I began asking myself some questions about
how we keep following the flow of the early Church
pattern. It was precipitated by looking at how we helped
new believers become integrated into the life of the
church; how we helped them to get to know what was
happening in the life of the church, who was who, what
ministries they could plug into. I found that our follow-
up team was worn out following up people that were not
that interested. I thought, 'The flow is all wrong.' I went
back to the Word of God looking for some evidence of
follow-up programs and I couldn't find any. So where was
the follow-up program for the three thousand people that
got saved on the day of Pentecost? If there was ever an
opportunity for God to teach us about how to follow
people up, it should be here. Surely three thousand
converts in one day would need to be supported by a
major follow-up strategy to make sure they were all
integrated into the church? In fact the early Church knew

nothing of elaborate, costly, demanding, high-energy
follow-up programs. Why? Because follow-up in the Bible
is the opposite to follow-up here in the twenty-first
century where we have lost much of the early Church
dynamics. New believers saw the devotion of the believers
before they came to salvation. They knew what they were
signing up for. It wasn't fudged or glossed over; they
were made aware of the costs involved beforehand.

The modern Church is riddled with contra-flows
instead of God's flow! And we wonder why we are
struggling, expending so much energy doing things that
should be happening instinctively. We need to get back
to the right model and break some of our unhealthy
thinking and behavioral patterns. In the New Testament,
Jesus never followed anyone up. What actually happened
was this: they followed Him up. He didn't get their
address, they got His address. He didn't get their phone
number, they got His phone number!

Look at this classic example: If ever there was a person
needing follow-up, it was the guy they called 'Legion'
(Mark 5:9). This guy was in a real mess. He had terrorized
the neighborhood for years as a demoniac, so surely he
would need quite a lot of counseling at least? He surely
needed 'deprogramming' and checking out to make sure
he was safe – to make sure all of those demons were out?
We find him clinging to Jesus, begging to go with Him,
but Jesus says, 'Get out of here. Go back to the town that
you terrorized and just tell them what God has done
for you.' Now what kind of follow-up is that? Jesus set
him loose because He believed that if the man was saved,
he was saved. Whatever happened to 'saved'? In the
western Church we have diluted 'saved'; we have added
to it in case it's not enough. We need to remind
ourselves that Jesus, all by Himself, is enough!

Jesus' approach, it seems, was the opposite to ours. He
didn't try to corral new believers and press them into

getting involved. Don't get me wrong, we believe in the courtesies of getting people's details and welcoming them into the life of the church. The difference is this: our follow-up must not spring from a fear that they won't come back but from a faith that if they are saved they will want to come back and get involved. We want to so inspire and attract them by the way we 'do' church – full of life and commitment – that there will be no stopping them coming back! There's a big difference.

Personally I'm still waiting to be followed-up – and that was over 30 years ago! Anybody else? Any day now I'm sure I'm going to get the phone call. Statistically speaking I shouldn't even be here! Why? Because I didn't get the attention that most new believers expect to get when they join a church – nor did many others who are still going strong for God today. I was saved out of an un-churched, heathen background. God saved me at the age of fifteen at school through the witness of a school-teacher. I just got plucked out of this heathen family. I couldn't go home and get any help; I couldn't go home and open my Bible, I didn't have a Bible. I had no help; no telephone, no transport, no godly influences in the home to encourage me to follow through. I had nothing and no one followed me up. So, what did I do? I set out to find other people like me in the town where I lived. I went to every meeting I could and discovered as much as I could by reading and talking to people. I went to every meeting I could possibly sneak into – the Deacons meeting, the Elders meeting, the Financial Trustees meeting, even the Women's meeting!

Wherever they were I would track them down and turn up at the appropriate house and knock on the door. They'd open the door and say, 'Who are you?' and I'd say, 'I'm Paul. I've just become a believer and I heard there's a meeting here tonight.' 'Well, this one's not for you,' they would say. 'A meeting not for me? How can that be?' I was all by myself, just finding where God's people were and determined to get involved.

When I first got saved I was shocked by the attitude of other Christians and the kind of language they would use when they talked to me. People would say things like, 'Now you're a Christian Paul you *must* read your Bible you know ...' What was that all about? It was like they were assuming that I wouldn't want to read it, or that I would at least be very reluctant and need some persuasion. This kind of language is full of assumption – 'You really ought to pray ... you should be giving to the church ... you ought to share your faith with others ...'

I wish someone had taken a positive approach with me and said, 'Now you're saved you're going to want to devour the Bible, so here's three!' 'Now you're saved you are going to love to pray. Here are the dates and times of all the prayer meetings. See you there!' 'Now that you're saved you are going to want to give, this is what the Bible says about it and this is how we do it ...' This type of language is flowing with divine devotion; it is assuming the best, not the worst! It is watering the incorruptible seed, releasing our power to become.

Eventually I said to our own follow-up team, 'You know what? We ain't gonna do this any more. We will do what is necessary to let people just know what they need to know. We'll be courteous and helpful as much as we can, but I don't want any of our team chasing around after reluctant people wearing us out.' Now we look for the devotion within people. Is there a divine desire, a divine 'want to' concerning the things of God? If it isn't there, we are not going to force-feed them.

For a long time we were more devoted to people making it than they were themselves. But if you operate that way, then in six months time when you are forced to relax your efforts, they become lukewarm and begin to coast along instead of committing themselves to the life of the church. These people become high-maintenance Christians, surviving off other believers who keep giving them another push.

If you are seeking to establish a growing church and 'cross over' into your destiny, then you need to be aware of this for your continued growth and development. The church members need to be educated that if they see a brother or sister in need, the last thing they should do is to go and tell a leader! If they see someone in difficulty then they just need to go and see what they can do for them. You don't read in the Bible that someone spotted a problem and reported it to whoever was head of that particular department – the people just helped one another, it was organic, it was in their DNA. Reverse the flow! Don't get worn out doing what you should not be doing in the first place! It will bring a huge release.

Chapter 10

God's 'City of Refuge' Churches

Numbers 35

We now turn to the second facet of a 'crossing over' church that I want to examine with you. Recently the Lord showed me something significant whilst I was reading Numbers chapter 35. In this chapter we read of various 'cities of refuge' that God had established for people who were in trouble and needed help. Beginning in verse 6 we read,

> ' "Six of the towns you give the Levites will be cities of refuge, to which a person who has killed someone may flee. In addition, give them forty-two other towns. In all you must give the Levites forty-eight towns, together with their pasture-lands. The towns you give the Levites from the land the Israelites possess are to be given in proportion to the inheritance of each tribe: Take many towns from a tribe that has many, but few from one that has few." Then the LORD said to Moses: "Speak to the Israelites and say to them: 'When you cross the Jordan into Canaan, select some towns to be your cities of refuge, to which a person who has killed someone accidentally may flee. They will be places of refuge from the avenger, so that a person*

accused of murder may not die before he stands trial before the assembly. These six towns you give will be your cities of refuge Give three on this side of the Jordan and three in Canaan as cities of refuge. These six towns will be a place of refuge for Israelites, aliens and any other people living among them, so that anyone who has killed another accidentally can flee there.' ''   (Numbers 35:6–15)

The only other place where the Bible mentions these cities is in Joshua chapter 20:

'Then the LORD said to Joshua: "Tell the Israelites to designate the cities of refuge, as I instructed you through Moses, so that anyone who kills a person accidentally and unintentionally may flee there and find protection from the avenger of blood. When he flees to one of these cities, he is to stand in the entrance of the city gate and state his case before the elders of that city. Then they are to admit him into their city and give him a place to live with them. If the avenger of blood pursues him, they must not surrender the one accused, because he killed his neighbor unintentionally and without malice aforethought. He is to stay in that city until he has stood trial before the assembly and until the death of the high priest who is serving at that time. Then he may go back to his own home in the town from which he fled." '   (Joshua 20:1–6)

As the pastor of a local church for more than twenty years, and having traveled all around our nation and the world talking to different leaders, the truth is that real spiritual vitality is very patchy. There are 'pockets' of blessing and dynamic spiritual life here and there, but you sometimes have to travel a long way to find them. There are certain regions of the UK where you would have to drive a very long way to find a church that would be really relevant and would encourage and equip you. There are numbers of people at our own church who come every Sunday having driven for two or three hours. They spend more time in the car than they do in the meeting. We feel that it's a real sacrifice they're making, but they don't feel it's a sacrifice. They feel that what they receive on that day is enough to bless, strengthen and encourage them to make the journey worthwhile. We have a saying in our church that, 'The church alive is worth the drive!'

This is unusual for Britain. In America they don't think twice about getting on a freeway and driving for a couple of hours, but in Britain where we don't have such a church-going culture, and where Sunday is traditionally a day off, something must really be happening for people to do that. However, it's also an indictment on our country because it means people are saying, 'There are no good churches near me.' It is causing us to redefine what 'local church' means, because for many people, their church is not local any more. The geographical boundaries of church have begun to be blurred because people are saying, 'I don't think I want to die in this dry part of our nation. I don't want to go to such and such a church out of some false sense of loyalty because my parents went there. I want to be where there is life.' I am not advocating people leaving their churches if that is the local body where God has added them as we have already discussed, but I do believe that there is no point staying involved in something that is not going anywhere and is not showing any signs of changing in the near future. There is no virtue in that. You are accountable for your own life before God.

City of refuge churches in our nation

I believe that we are living in critical times. There is a sense of urgency in my spirit to press forward into all that God has for us as His Church. All of us should have a sense of urgency not to allow ourselves to be held back by counterproductive relationships, negative mindsets and attitudes, but to press into all that God is calling us to. To this end, I believe that God showed me there are 'city of refuge' churches in our own nation that He has established; churches that provide a haven for those who are looking for a 'safe place' or a second chance.

God has got 'city of refuge' churches scattered across the world. There were only six in the whole of the land that God gave the Israelites, but six was enough. God has begun to reveal His 'city of refuge' churches in our nation and I believe that He has called our church to be one of them. 'Can any good thing come out of Bradford?' people have asked. Plenty of negative stuff has come out of our city, but now I believe that God wants to put us and others on the map as a source of hope for our nation – the hope that things can be different. If you don't currently see yourself, or your church, as one of God's cities of refuge, then maybe things need to change. It could be a case of 'watch this space.'

Refuge churches are an oasis of life in a land that is spiritually dry. They are places of escape and restoration for spiritually desperate people who are fleeing to find life, to find food, to find help. They are places that will understand the plight of these fugitives and provide relief. They are places that won't try to define you by your past, but will accept you for who you are. We are known in our city as 'the church that doesn't care'. We don't care where you've been, what you've done, what your postcode is or what your reputation is. Abundant Life Church is 'Second Chance Central'. The moment you arrive here and get saved, you start with a clean slate. The biblical cities of refuge were communities that didn't define people by their past. These cities were based on the concept of expressing the heart of God for the fugitives, the misunderstood, the disenfranchised and the outcasts of society. They were places of restoration, refreshing and re-focussing for lives that would otherwise have been lost. These cities were not earned in battle, they were gifts from God. It was God's idea. They were grace gifts from God to people in the nation because He knew that one day they would be needed.

One day, people in your region are going to need a church like yours. God doesn't wait until there's a demand to provide a supply. God doesn't work like people. People hedge their bets. If there is a demand then they will increase their stock. God doesn't wait until He sees a demand and then think, 'Oh, I better do something.' God always plans ahead and creates a supply way in advance of the demand. He caused Joseph to be twenty years ahead of the demand when he governed Pharaoh's Egypt. Don't define your church by what you see now. Your church is existing, growing, prospering, and relevant because of what's about to come, not because of what's already happened. There are thousands of people who don't know that you exist yet, but when God strikes our nation with spiritual famine, guess where they're going to look? Not to some dead, dull, boring, irrelevant church that hasn't moved on for years and has no intention of doing – they're going to run in their thousands to cities of refuge, to places that don't judge them, or point a finger at them. Our church has over 50 inner city outreach initiatives. So, the chances are you're going to come on Sunday morning and be sat next to a girl that works on the streets. You're going to come and sit next to people that don't look like you, dress like you, or smell like you. But we tell people, if you can't deal with that then you need to leave because we need your seat. This refuge spirit, this grace must be at the heart of the places that God, I believe, is designating in our country and across the world right now.

These cities of refuge were run by Levites; they were run by spiritual people, not by politicians or people trying to make a name for themselves, but priests. And these churches of refuge will be led and taken forward by spiritual people, by men and women of God who have no other agenda than the kingdom of God and His purposes. They must be people that have a love for others and a heart to build people into a cohesive family unit and an army who will spread the Gospel amongst those that they came from. The cities of refuge were run on different systems, by different rules and values than other cities, and likewise the churches of refuge. They will have very different values and a keener sense of what matters and what doesn't than most churches in our world. They will be places of life, joy and acceptance; places where you can't walk in and be there for more than a few seconds before people come and welcome you and love you and greet you and accept you and befriend you. I have visited churches in this country where nobody speaks to you. Not necessarily large churches either, but small churches. They are not cities of refuge, they are exclusive clubs for spiritual fat cats; they are religious retirement homes.

The only people who were born and raised in these cities of refuge were leaders. The only permanent residents were Levites and their families. Imagine churches where the only people who are raised there are leaders – leaders in life, in marriage, in business, leaders in character, leaders in morality, integrity and so on. Imagine raising a church full of leaders! I believe that every person in our church is destined to be a leader. Everybody in our church needs to be a leader in whatever sphere of life they are involved; people of influence in every sphere of life. Leaders were the hub, the core, the center of these cities of refuge, and when we grow leaders we can change our world.

Of the six cities of refuge mentioned in the Bible, three were to the west of the Jordan and three were to the east. In the west lay Kedesh, Shechem and Kiriath Arba or Hebron. The names of these cities are interesting. Their Hebrew names meaning the following: Kedesh means *sanctuary*, Shechem means *shoulders* and Kiriath Arba means *fellowship* or *joining*. In other words, these three cities were where the heavy-shouldered could go and find sanctuary, fellowship and refuge. To the east of the Jordan were Bezer, Ramoth and Golan. Bezer means *new strength*, Ramoth means *high value* and Golan means *exiles*. In other words these three cities were places where former exiles could come and find new strength and new value as God redefined them and restored their hope and dignity. God could put them back on their feet, put a new twinkle in their eye, allow them to put their shoulders back, hold their head up high and without shame eventually go back to where they came from. They went out a different person, carrying with them the spirit of refuge that once reached out to them.

Under Joshua and successive generations, a road system was built and signs were erected to make the cities of refuge easier to find and easier to get to. This needs to happen in our nation too. Some of these cities of refuge are there, but God hasn't put a signpost up yet. The timing of God's signpost will be determined by your response and readiness to what God wants you to do. Are you ready to receive such needy people? You know one of the devil's greatest strategies is *containment*. The devil is not half as bothered about pushing you back as he is about holding you where you are. He doesn't need for you to start backsliding and quit, to start doing stupid things. He just needs to press the pause button and put you on hold. That will do fine. In fact, that's more dangerous than if you quit and go back so that every-body can obviously see that you're out of business. To still be 'trading', but not in anything that really matters is more useful to the enemy than if you shut down.

Once when I returned from a trip to the States our plane circled for over an hour, but I didn't know it until afterwards. You can circle for an awfully long time and still think you're flying in a straight line, it will be barely perceptible. You can be circling in your church and not know it too. Israel circled for forty years on what was supposed to be a two-week flight! Eventually you become aware of it – 'You know, I think I've seen this before . . .' – but by then you've already wasted a huge amount of time.

God is beginning to erect signs and create ways of finding these places in the world. I believe it is time for them to be designated and identified. We are in desperate need of them. They are churches that have crossed over and are doing God's business, working to extend His Kingdom, creating places of refuge, love and acceptance; giving people a second chance. We believe that God has called us to be such a church. Could he be calling your church too?

PART 5

Moving Forward, Leaving a Legacy

Chapter 11

Tranquility Breeds Creativity

1 Chronicles 22:6–10

The time came when Joshua and Israel crossed over into their land of promise. And your time will come too. Equipped with the principles for individuals, leaders and churches we have explored so far, you will press over your Jordan and then face the thrilling challenge of establishing and enlarging your God-given territory. It is to these matters I now want to turn in our two final chapters. I want to deal with how we can move on to possess more of the promised land that God has helped us to occupy, and how we can leave a lasting legacy for future generations.

In this chapter we will examine an aspect of the life of King Solomon, the wisest man who ever lived, because he is uniquely placed to teach us something very special about how we should live once we are through the challenges that accompany the actual process of crossing over.

Solomon was the son of King David and succeeded him as king. All his life David had been a warrior king. He had always known some kind of warfare. If he wasn't fighting one battle, he was fighting another; if he was at rest, he was only at rest between enemies and was simply regrouping in order to go out and fight again. From the day he killed Goliath until the day he died, David was battling enemies. By the end of his life, finally peace reigned, albeit a peace won through continuous conflict, and he was at last able to hand on to his son Solomon, a new beginning.

In fact, the name Solomon means 'peace'. David gave a name to Solomon that would be characteristic of his reign. The season of warfare had passed and the time for peace had come. This thought is encapsulated in the following verses from 1 Chronicles 22:

> *'Then he* [David] *called for his son Solomon and charged him with building a house for the* Lord, *the God of Israel. David said to Solomon: "My son, I had it in my heart to build a house for the Name of the* Lord *my God. But this word of the* Lord *came to me: 'You have shed much blood and have fought many wars. You are not to build a house for my Name ... But you will have a son who will be a man of peace ... I will give him rest from all his enemies ... I will grant Israel peace and quiet during his reign. He is the one who will build a house for my Name.'"'*
>
> (1 Chronicles 22:6–10)

Different leadership for different seasons

There are different kinds of leadership for different times and seasons. Sometimes, one kind of leadership is not the best kind for a particular season. There is a leadership style that is built for war. Winston Churchill was like that. Certain leaders are built for crises, moments of danger and high drama; they know how to fight. But then there are times when it is a season of peace and during that time a different type of leadership is needed –

a leadership that knows how to build. God acknow-
ledged that David was a warlike leader. He was a warrior
King and there was no one like him in all the history of
the Hebrew nation. But for that reason God told him
that he was not the one to build God's house. He wasn't
a building leader, he was a warring leader. So God asked
him to give up the desire of his heart and to issue a
mandate to his son to build God's house. God made
Solomon to be a man of peace. Solomon's leadership was
made for a different kind of administration. He had a
completely different anointing from his father David; a
completely different leadership commissioning. His job
was going to be to restore an infrastructure that had been
broken down by generations of warfare.

Examine where you are on your journey as a church –
ask yourselves, 'What season are we in at the moment?
What time is it, spiritually, for us as a church?' Sometimes churches will go through seasons of 'internal' war,
where just like in the early Church the enemy tries to
sabotage the church from within. At such times you may
find yourself dealing with divisiveness, issues of control,
manipulation, church politics, and so on. Following such
times there will be unprecedented peace and harmony,
and during those times you must be prepared to build,
working towards establishing all that is in your heart.

In times of peace, it is possible to achieve more in a
single year than you achieved in the previous ten. New
ministries can be launched, finances generated, build-
ings built, people reached. In times of peace, you can
maximize your productivity. This is not the same during
wartime. What's the point of building anything if it's
going to be bombed the next week? Why build something if the enemy will immediately raid and rob it?
During wartime you don't build much, but rather focus
on defeating your enemies and establishing the basis for
a better future.

Peace = creativity

It is not hard to figure out that the major time of growth for any church takes place during the 'building' seasons, not the 'battling' seasons, though both are necessary seasons in church life. We must fight for peace when the season demands it, because during peace we will grow more rapidly – hence the title of this chapter, *tranquility breeds creativity*. This is what Solomon discovered. In the season of peace and quiet, creativity can explode and productivity can reach its maximum potential. You are at your most creative when you are at your most tranquil.

This principle can be applied to your personal life as well as church life. Whatever you do in life – your work, career, ministry – will not work well if you are stressed out and under pressure. When you are stressed and anxious you are not creative, but when you are tranquil – at peace and restful, then you are at your most creative because you have space to think, to dream, to plan.

When you work from a place of tranquility and peace, you will be amazed at the flow of creativity that follows. During this time of tranquility Solomon's own creativity exploded. We are told he wrote 3,000 proverbs, 1,005 songs and encyclopedias about plant life, birds, insects and reptiles (1 Kings 4:32–33). When you are constantly in the midst of battle you are too busy looking over your shoulder to be creative; you are too busy with your enemies to be at peace and get into a creative flow.

Tranquility means: to be cool, restful, serene, unruffled, unperturbed. *Creativity* means: cleverness, fertility, imagination, inventiveness, originality, talent, resourcefulness and vision. When we are restful, we are clever; when we are serene, we are fertile; when we are unruffled, we become inventive; when we are unperturbed, we become resourceful.

We can see this principle played out in the life of Isaac as he went about re-digging the wells that belonged to his father Abraham (Genesis 26). The Philistines had blocked them up and every time he tried to unblock one he was resisted by them. He couldn't make any progress and so he was forced to move on and he gave names to the wells that spoke of conflict, confrontation and resistance. God instructed him to keep moving on and to keep digging because He was going to make room for him somewhere. Eventually Isaac came to a place where he was left in peace and there was no resistance. The Bible says he called that place Rehoboth which means 'God made room for us' and he said, 'Here we will flourish.' God gave Isaac tranquility which eventually exploded into creativity. What he planted came up a hundred-fold. His crops, his goods, his cattle and his belongings just reproduced exponentially. Multiplication was on his life. Why? Because he had peace. There was no resistance to his blessing. He just dug that well and the water came gushing up. He put his roots down there because that's what you did in Isaac's day, you lived around water. Isaac said, 'God has blessed me with my own well of blessing. It's a gusher of productivity.'

Protecting your peace

We also need to be aware that there is a flip side to this principle. The Apostle Paul warned us, 'Don't be ignorant of how the devil operates.' Tranquility produces creativity, but unrest – the absence of peace – produces division. We need to understand this and protect our tranquility in order to maintain our creativity. If we relax and just assume that peace will continue then we unwittingly invite unrest into our lives. It is interesting that what follows unrest is not an immediate loss of creativity, but division. The devil does not wage an all out assault on your creativity, he begins in a much more subtle way than that by creating division. That which is divided can no longer work together; it loses its purpose and focus.

In the church setting, the devil knows that bringing division will begin to stem productivity down the line. So he begins to sow unrest. It could be someone on the phone saying things to you that they shouldn't be saying, sowing discord. That's where unrest begins – if you don't squash it right there it begins to ferment. Unrest enters your church with a 'smile' and then begins to erode the peace and tranquility. If that division is not dealt with, then the creativity and productivity will quickly dry up.

The challenge for each one of us personally is how we make our contribution to church life in the light of this. You have a decision to make. Are you going to contribute to the peace and tranquility with your words, your serving, in your attitude, your relationships, your commitment? Are you going to be a sower of peace or discord? Make it your aim to infect people with tranquility. Be a carrier of tranquility, so that you bring the calm and peace of God into every situation. People should not be ruffled or perturbed by our presence, they should feel serene. When you arrive at a 'scene' in your church, do you throw water on it, or do you throw petrol on it? If you come across a divisive element in your church, do you speak words that bring peace or do you help make a bigger blaze? Instead of inflaming a situation, be a carrier of the tranquility and peace of Christ.

The challenge comes to us as a church to be in peace and harmony with other groups of believers around us. If there is unrest then we will be discordant. If we are distressed about certain things then we will be disagreeable. When it comes to church unity, we have often majored on the minors. We have scrutinized the differences between us instead of recognizing what we have in common. When you begin to really examine it, believers of every variety and persuasion still have more things in common than things that divide them. We have a lot in common. Not things like social interests or material possessions or any of that stuff which is unimportant, but our oneness in Christ, our belief in the irrefutable truths of the Bible rather than minor theological disputes.

It is like having a great marriage that stands the test of time. The marriages that survive the longest are not the ones that have no disagreements. They may have just as many, if not more disagreements than a marriage that fails. The difference is that they have made a choice, a decision, to focus on those things that they agree about more than they focus on those things they disagree about. It is a determination to maintain peace and tranquility that arises from focusing on unifying issues and giving no place to division.

There is room in every church for 'difference'. We shouldn't mind each other's differences, we should celebrate them. Some people like short hair, some people like long hair; some people are fat, some people are thin; some people are tall, some people are short. We have black people, white people, young and old; people who are better off and some people who are less well off; people who drive expensive cars, and people who drive cars that you push more than you drive. The church has professional people – doctors, lawyers and architects, and people who are gifted at more manual tasks. There are people with all kinds of gifts and talents. We need to celebrate those differences. Our differences only become a problem if they begin to cost us our unity. We can celebrate our differences if our foundation of unity is sound, and our unity is not found in our culture, our class, our creed, our social upbringing, or our color. Our unity is in Christ who is not black or white, male or female, Jewish or Greek, rich or poor – He's just Christ.

Where does peace come from?

Here's an important question. Where does peace come from? 'Peace comes from God' I hear you say. Well, how come a lot of Christians have no peace then? There must be something else going on here that we're missing. If that were true and there were no other conditions needed for peace to come, then we wouldn't have so many Christians on anti-depressants and tranquilizers. Why can't so many Christians sleep at night? Why do so many Christians live on their nerve ends? Here's what I believe most of God's people are missing when it comes to understanding peace. Isaiah 32:17 says,

> *'The fruit of righteousness will be peace;*
> *the effect of righteousness will be quietness*
> *and confidence for ever.'*

Peace is a by-product of righteousness. What is righteousness? Righteousness simply means *doing right*. That's it. Righteousness is doing right. The fruit of doing right will be peace. If you do what's right in God's eyes then peace will be in your life. Forget about doing what is popular, or what is right in the eyes of others. Do what's right according to the will of God and you will be blessed with peace. If you will do right, the Word of God *guarantees* that the fruit will be peace.

The Bible says that the effect of doing right will be quietness and confidence forever. If you want to be more confident in your life, then do right. Righteousness will give you an overwhelming, abiding sense of confidence.

Confidence comes from knowing that you are right with God and that you are walking in the bulls-eye of God's will for your life. Confidence comes from knowing all is well with your soul before God. That will give you incredible confidence. Doing what's right produces peace, peace produces tranquility, and tranquility produces creativity.

In Psalm 85:10, David writes,

> *'Love and faithfulness meet together;*
> *righteousness and peace kiss each other.'*

He uses this wonderful poetic language to describe this principle. Righteousness and peace go together, they are an item! What an amazing picture. Fight off your enemies when you have to, but make sure that your focus is to gain peace and tranquility. Then, all that you desire to do for God can begin to happen as you flow forth in creativity, enjoying the blessing of God.

Chapter 12

Live Full but Die Empty

2 Kings 13:20

Now that we have crossed over and faced all the challenges that it brings, we have a further ongoing challenge. In fact, when you are living for God the challenges never stop! You mustn't ever become complacent or think that you have made it. We will never have 'arrived' until we reach Heaven. So, in this chapter I want to issue a challenge to you, a challenge to 'live full and die empty'. It is this challenge that will leave a lasting legacy to bless the future generations.

Recently I was struck by a very odd verse in 2 Kings. It is one of those verses in the Bible that stands out to us as being quite peculiar, and yet no explanation for it is given. There is nothing in the context of the verse, either before or after it, that explains why it is there. It simply says:

> *'Elisha died and was buried. Now Moabite raiders used to enter the country every spring. Once while some Israelites were burying a man, suddenly they saw a band of raiders; so they threw the man's body into Elisha's tomb. When the body touched Elisha's bones, the man came to life and stood up on his feet.'* (2 Kings 13:20)

Although this incident is not elaborated upon, it must be in the Bible for some reason since all the Word of God is inspired and useful for our instruction (2 Timothy 3:16). I believe that locked up in Elisha's bones, even years after the rest of his body had decayed, was a reservoir of incredible power. It was impressive power, not least because the Bible tells us it represented a double portion of the power that was given to Elijah. We are talking about perhaps one of the greatest Old Testament anointings that any human being ever possessed.

The Bible records that Elisha had died and was buried in a tomb. Years afterwards a band of raiders sweep into the area, just as some Israelites are burying a friend. Instead of finishing the burial they say to each other, 'We'll leave him and come back later. Drop the body in that old tomb for now.' So they did, not knowing that when they came back later he wouldn't be there! As soon as the dead man hit Elisha's bones there was an incredible release of power that was enough to blast him back to life. He stood up on his feet and walked out of his own funeral.

The king of that time, Jehoash, was spiritually dull. The nation was overwhelmed by enemies and they could have done with even a small percentage of the power that was resident in those bones. I asked the Lord, 'How was it that Elisha could be long dead, yet the great power you invested in him was still hanging around in his bones in the grave?' How could power stay in bones? The Holy Spirit spoke this phrase to me: 'Elisha died before he could get empty.'

Releasing bottled up potential

For years we've had a wrong theology. Our theology has been, 'Live a full life and die full at a ripe old age.' We've got it wrong.

By the time we die, we've read all the right books, listened to all the right tapes, gone to all the right meetings and conferences. Why? To gather more information, get a better theology, become more gifted, be more blessed. I'm not against any of those things, but the truth is this: we've been there, done that, got the T-shirt and still the church is contained and the world unreached. If only a fraction of what God has put inside your life could be spilled out to the people you work with, your friends, your family, all those who touch your life, they would be blown away.

You may not think that you are especially gifted or talented, but God can use you just as much as any other person. Look at the guy who was blind and Jesus healed him. He went around preaching to others after that amazing event and do you know what his message was? 'I was blind, but now I can see.' He didn't even have three points in his sermon. If all you know about God is that you were blind and now you can see, then just go out and tell people that.

Why was that power locked up in those bones? Because what God gives you for earth cannot go back to heaven. It has to be used up here. Elisha had gone, but his power could not go with him. His power was a gift from God that was to be used to help people, to break yokes, to bring the Word of God to the nation, to perform miracles, signs and wonders, and to be God's prophetic voice in his time and season. That power had no use in heaven. In heaven there is no need for prophecy; no need for the sick to be healed; no need for the lost to be reached, or the dead raised, or demons cast out. All that power was intended to be spent on the earth. Elisha died before he could get rid of it all and there it was, still hanging around in his bones.

You can only spend your gifts, your calling, your abilities – the miracle of God that is stored up in you –

here and now on the earth. This is it. It's not a rehearsal. You are not getting ready to spend it, you have got to get rid of this stuff now and fast. If God told you that tonight that you were going to die, what would you have to do, who would you have to speak to, where would you need to go to start getting rid of stuff that you know you've been holding on to when you should have been giving it away? God says to you, 'Start doing it and start doing it right now.' You've got to live full, but the idea is to get empty before you go to heaven.

It is God's intention for us that we live full, but living full is not about acquiring more and more for ourselves until we are stuffed with fullness; living full is actually about getting empty! The destination of all fullness has always been emptiness. God is drawn to emptiness. He is looking for empty people, for empty vessels. If you want to attract the presence of God then you need to keep emptying yourself out into other needy people.

The greatest energy crisis in the world today is the enormous reservoir of God-given power that exists inside believers that is being contained instead of being released. Every believer has this same potential locked up within them. We all start off the same and then somehow we allow life to bring containment after containment upon us. The result is that you walk around with gifts bottled up inside you. Bottled gifts, bottled destiny, bottled dreams and visions, bottled courage and faith. It's all bottled up within you and the cork's not coming out. You are full up and you need to get empty. You've simply got to get out what's inside you.

I believe that God is so committed to getting out of you what He put into you, that if necessary, He will come and turn you upside down to do it. He will turn you upside down and shake that cork out of you if He has to. Look at what God did with Jonah in order to release the power he had locked up inside himself. He had to send a storm to disturb the ship Jonah was running away on, have him thrown overboard and have a whale swallow him. Now that's drastic! The storm was only a little bit of trouble to get Jonah ready for the real trouble. Jonah was inside the whale for three days, and the Bible tells us that he said, 'Oh God, I will fulfil my vow to thee.' I bet he did! I expect God responded to Jonah by saying, 'You know Jonah, we really didn't need to do this?' God is saying to His Church today, 'We don't need to keep doing this. We don't need all this fuss and mess. We don't need these storms every few months. Just do what I've asked you to do.'

I want to enter heaven empty. I want to get there absolutely bone dry. Nothing left to say, no one left to help; nowhere left to go; no money in the bank. Even Bill Gates has realized that you can't take it with you and has started giving millions to educating the next generation. I want to stand before God and have nothing outstanding. Some people say that they want to die preaching. I don't. I just want to have that inner assurance that both Jesus and the Apostle Paul had that I've finished my race.

The Bible reveals that Elisha tried to get empty. He tried to pour himself into his servant, Gehazi, but his heart was not right. God couldn't establish Elisha's legacy through Gehazi so it remained inside Elisha. At the end of his life Elisha was sick. He eventually died of this sickness and I guess he must have known that he was going to die. When King Jehoash came to visit him near the end of his life, Elisha was still trying to empty himself. He tells the spiritually dull Jehoash, to bring a bow and arrows to him. He gets the king to put an arrow in the bow and give it to him. Do you see what he is doing? He's trying to get rid of his power. Elisha put his hands on the hands of the king and they shot the arrow together. The king was so dull that he didn't know what was going on. Elisha said, 'Behold the arrow of the Lord's

victory over the Arameans.' He was trying to do something to leave a legacy for his people – a victory over
God's enemies. The king still didn't get the plot, so
Elisha said, 'Get me the arrows that are left.' The king
gets the arrows and Elisha tells him to strike the ground
with them. Elisha could see something in the Spirit that
the king could not see. Perhaps he could see many future
victories for the Lord's people with each strike of the
ground. The king still couldn't see it. He felt embarrassed
to perform this prophetic sign, so he tapped the ground
three times and thought, 'That's probably enough to
satisfy this crazy guy.' But Elisha rebuked him saying,
'You fool, you should have hit the ground five, six, eight,
or nine times. Can't you see I'm trying to get empty
before I die and leave a deposit of my power to future
generations of Israel?'

The ultimate living full and dying empty was Jesus on
the cross. He was in agony, with hardly a breath left in
His body, and yet even in that terrible moment He
finds the strength to say, 'Father, there's a man next to
me who is close to your kingdom. If you will give me
strength for one last sinner I will snatch him from the
jaws of hell. There's room for one more before I die, just
one more ... ' He turned His head to this man and said,
'Today, you will be with me in paradise' (Luke 23:43).
When Jesus said, *'It is finished!'* He meant, mission
accomplished, there's nothing left for Me to do or say. I
came full and am leaving empty.

Leaving a legacy

I have often wondered in my life – as I have struggled
and fought with things in ministry – whether I was really
meant to be fighting them. I don't think they were all
supposed to be my battles. I think some of the stuff that I

have wrestled with I inherited because my forefathers did not die empty. They didn't tackle some things before they died and they left it for another generation to fight. I have the overwhelming feeling sometimes, 'Lord, this is not my battle. A previous generation should have beaten this, but they didn't for whatever reason.' They didn't beat it, so around it comes again, the Goliath they didn't kill now threatens their children. I have promised my spiritual children I will never ever hand them a giant that I was supposed to beat. If every generation defeated their own giants, what an incredible legacy they would leave the emerging generation.

Crossing over leaders, individuals and churches live full but never stockpile their fullness. They constantly give away their excess life to empty people. Our old church was full of itself; we were blessed, content, happy and helping no one. Our new 'crossed over' church is pouring its life into the city, we are holding nothing back. We are determined to leave no power locked up in our bones. We are living full and intend to die empty.

Epilogue

Thousands of churches are yet to 'cross over' and millions of people depend on them doing so. Like the Reubenites, Gadites and half-tribe of Mannaseh (Joshua 1:12–14), I am committed to helping all my brethren 'possess all their lands' and everything else God has for their future, before I fully settle into enjoying my own.

Rise up Joshua! Wherever you are and whoever you are. Be courageous and strong. Take as many of God's people over with you as possible. For this is our time and this is our turn. I'll look out for you on the other side.

If you have enjoyed this book and would like to help us to send a copy of it and many other titles to needy pastors in the **Third World**, please write for further information or send your gift to:

**Sovereign World Trust
PO Box 777, Tonbridge
Kent TN11 0ZS
United Kingdom**

or to the '**Sovereign World**' distributor in your country.

Visit our website at **www.sovereign-world.org**
for a full range of Sovereign World books.